Phonics
in Lessons, Pictures,
and Activities

James W. Forgan, Ph.D.
Florida Atlantic University

Harry W. Forgan, Ph.D.
University of Miami

Illustrated by
Amy O'Brien Krupp

Good Year Books
An Imprint of Pearson Learning

Good Year Books are available for most basic curriculum subjects plus many enrichment areas. For more Good Year Books, contact your local bookseller or educational dealer. For a complete catalog with information about other Good Year Books, please write:

Good Year Books
Pearson Learning
299 Jefferson Road
Parsippany, NJ 07054

Book design by Amy O'Brien Krupp.
Copyright © 2000 Harry W. Forgan and James W. Forgan.
All Rights Reserved.
Printed in the United States of America.

0-673-58904-8

1 2 3 4 5 6 7 8 9—ML—08 07 06 05 04 03 02 01 00

Preface

This book is for teachers, parents, and tutors who want to help children sound out words. Information is provided to help you (a) learn the sounds in the English language, (b) learn guidelines for teaching phonics, (c) test students to determine what to teach, and (d) teach children phonics using the 48 lesson plans in this book. If you want practical information and ready-to-use ideas for teaching phonics, this book is for you.

Many of the ideas in this book were first published in a 1978 book called *Phorgan's Phonics*, written by Harry W. Forgan, Ph.D., and illustrated by Bonnie Flint Striebel. Though very successful, the book was taken out of print when phonics instruction was neglected for a period of time.

Many teachers and parents requested a new edition of *Phorgan's Phonics* and this book, *Phonics in Lessons, Pictures, and Activities*, is the result. I asked my son, Dr. Jim Forgan, to work with me to update the ideas and create new activities. The emphasis here is on a balanced approach to reading instruction, the major goal of which is to help children "unlock" words so they can more fully comprehend and enjoy what they are learning.

Jim and I would like to thank our family members and friends for their cooperation and support. We dedicate this book to Jim and Peggy's children, Emily and Teddy, and to Jennifer and Temple's daughter Kali Kessinger, in hopes that they will learn phonics and enjoy many stories.

Table of Contents

PART I

Getting Ready to Teach Phonics

How to Get the Most Out of This Book

We believe there are five steps to follow to get the most out of this book:

First

Begin by reading "Ten Tips to Remember When Teaching Phonics." You will be more effective if you follow these guidelines, which provide practical suggestions to help children use phonics.

Second

Read the suggestions for using the 48 lesson plans in this book. Each lesson plan suggests a motivational way to introduce the sound, a reinforcement activity to practice the sound, and activities for "Working with Words" to help children learn the sound using a multimethod strategy. The first two parts of this lesson plan (introducing and reinforcing) might be used over a period of two days, while the activities for "Working with Words" can be used repeatedly.

Third

Peruse the section titled "Sounds in the English Language" if you need to review or learn about the sounds. Pictures of key words are provided to help you.

Fourth

Read how to assess children's use of phonics by surveying the tests and actually administering some of the tests to children.

Fifth

Select and use the lesson plans that are appropriate for your children. You can refer back to the sequence that is suggested in "Ten Tips to Remember When Teaching Phonics," use the results of your assessment, or follow any curriculum guide that suggests sounds to teach. Have phun!

Ten Tips to Remember When Teaching Phonics

1. *Most—not all—words in the English language can be "sounded out."* There is disagreement about which rules of phonics apply, but generally eight out of ten words (80 percent) can be sounded out. Twenty percent have no rhyme or reason according to principles of phonics; these must be memorized. Simply tell children the English language is made up of words from different languages so some words are not spelled as they sound. Show the children some of the following words, which are not spelled as they sound. Ask the children to "sound out" the words and then say them normally. Children—and parents—will soon learn that phonics is not the total answer for recognizing words. Some must be memorized, and readers can use the context, dictionary, and other techniques to recognize the words.

to	two	shall	two
of	what	most	ready
you	who	buy	visit
have	said	both	great
one	some	put	today
bread	give	does	move
do	eight	shoes	very
color	come	was	friend
woman	get	want	above

2. *Letters have two qualities.* Help children realize that letters usually have two qualities—a name and a sound (or sounds). For example, say the following names and sounds.

Name		Sound	
b	(bee)	/b/	as in *ball*
c	(see)	/k/	as in *cat*
		or /s/	as in *circle*
d	(dee)	/d/	as in *dog*

Make clear to children that letters have names and that each letter represents one or more sounds. As children sound out words, be sure they are saying the sounds rather than the letter name. Knowing that *b* represents /b/ helps you sound out a word such as *ball*. If you say the letter names, you will not be able to sound out the word. (Of course the long vowel sounds do sound exactly like the names of the letters: Āpes ēat Īce ōver Ūtah.)

3. *Look for sound patterns.* Teach children to look for sound patterns rather than to sound out each letter. Some letters appear together frequently and actually form a pattern—a combination of individual sounds into one sound, such as:

an   en   in   ill

It is much easier to sound out words if you blend a few sounds together rather than speak several individual sounds. For example, if you were going to sound out *perambulate*, you would look at the patterns with *er*, *am*, and *ate*, rather than saying the sound of each letter.

This	Not this
per am bu late	/p/e/r/a/mb/u/l/a/te

Sound patterns help you know what the vowel sounds are and make it easier to pronounce the words.

4. *Develop a listening vocabulary.* Children must have a large listening vocabulary—words they hear and understand—before phonics is useful.

If children sound out a word they have not heard, phonics does not help with word comprehension at all. For example, try to sound out the word *philtrum*.

You probably said *filltrum* by recognizing *ph* represents /f/, *il* as in *fill*, and *trum* is like *drum*. You may have successfully used phonics, but unless you have heard the word before, you wouldn't know that the *philtrum* is the part of your face located directly under your nose and before your lips. The reader must use phonics in combination with other word-recognition techniques, such as using a dictionary or sentence context, to determine the meaning of the word.

5. *See the letter.* When learning sound/symbol associations, children must *see* the letter in addition to hearing the sound. Be sure to write

the grapheme (letter or letters) that represent the phoneme (sound). When teaching /d/, be sure the children notice *d* and begin to associate *d* with /d/. Likewise, when teaching sound patterns such as *all*, be sure the children look at *all* as they say /all/. Phonics is nothing more than making associations between written symbols and sounds—that is why it is imperative that the learners *look* at the letter as they *say* the sound.

6. *See the words in context.* Children must see the words they are learning in sentences (context) rather than in isolation. Many of the reinforcement activities in this book present the sounds (words) the children are learning on game boards or activity sheets. For example, the reinforcement activity for /l/ is a game called "Ladders and Loops."

Children enjoy playing this game because they get to move ahead if they land on a "lucky ladder" and move back if they land on a "lousy loop." Meanwhile they have many opportunities to read words that begin with the /l/ sound, such as *lay*, *lost*, *learn*, *line*, *left*, *late*, *love*, *ladies*, *lunch*, *like*, *little*, and *large*. Teachers who use this game wisely will have children look at all the words and notice how they begin with the letter *l*, which sounds like /l/. Do not teach phonics in isolation, but rather help children apply the knowledge about the sound to real-world reading.

7. *Don't overexaggerate the letter sounds.* When teaching sounds, it is permissible to exaggerate the sound but then say the word normally. For example, if you are teaching the sound /d/ as in *dog*, it is okay to say, "d-og." But then put the /d/ and the /og/ together to from a meaningful word—*dog.* Talk with the children about their dogs as you concentrate on your major objective—helping them associate /d/ with *d.* Do not have the children say, "/d/ /d/ /d/ /d/, dog." Saying /d/ one time and combining it with /og/ is sufficient.

8. *Use particular grapheme–phoneme associations.* In addition to teaching children to associate graphemes and phonemes—symbols and sounds—it is important to teach children that a particular grapheme-letter will represent a certain sound. Remember, in the English language 26 letters represent 45 sounds. Some letters, especially the vowels, represent many different sounds. If you are teaching children long *a* as in *ape,* tell them when *a* is likely to represent the long *a* sound. For example, you will teach children to say long *a* when:

a and *y* are together as in:

clay	pay	play	way
hay	gray	spray	say
may	tray	day	lay

a and *i* are together as in:

| aid | paint | maid |

| main | drain | rain |
| brain | pain | bait |

a is in a word or syllable with the final *e* (CVCE) as in:

race	case	brace
safe	space	cage
ate	age	name
rake	game	take

Do not just teach children that the letter *a* can sound like /a/, but also teach them the letter combinations that represent long *a*—*ai, ay,* and CVCE.

9. *There is no magical sequence for teaching the consonant sounds of the English language.* Children generally learn the sounds in their own names and friends' names first. Popular words, such as McDonald's and Burger King, can also be used to teach sound-symbol associations.

You can administer tests to determine which sounds to teach first, but we generally recommend teaching the consonant sounds and some common vowel sounds first as well as sound patterns that these letter combinations can form.

A word of caution: Avoid teaching sounds in alphabetical order simply because the vowel represents so many sounds. If you begin by teaching *a,* which one of the six sounds that *a* represents are you going to teach: *a* as in *ape, apple, are, care, banana,* or *ball*? It is better to teach by frequently appearing consonant sounds such as *b* and *t* first, and then introduce some long and short vowel sounds.

10. *Teach strategy instead of rules.* Do not teach too many rules, but rather teach students a strategy to identify unknown words.

A Word Recognition Strategy—3SR

Teach students a strategy or a series of steps to follow to identify unknown words. Since phonics is not the only way to recognize words, be sure to teach children to use phonics as *one* step in their word-recognition strategy. Phonics is best used in combination with other techniques, including:

1. **Skip** the unknown word and continue reading. Help children realize good readers do not stop but rather continue reading to get the meaning. The essence of reading is getting the meaning—not just recognizing the words. It is possible to get some meaning without calling or pronouncing each word.

2. Try to **sound** out the word by looking for phonograms or sound patterns.

3. Analyze the **structure** of the word. If it is a long word (six or more letters), perhaps the unknown word is a compound word. See if you recognize two words in one or if there is a prefix or suffix that is making the word look different. Perhaps the word is a contraction.

4. Consult a **reference,** such as a dictionary or glossary, to learn both the pronunciation and meaning(s) of the unknown word.

You can teach children to remember these steps by telling them to use the 3SR strategy when they come to an unfamiliar word:

Skip the word—read on.

Sound out the word.

Structure clues—compound word, prefix, suffix, contraction

Reference—dictionary, glossary, knowledgeable person

Using the Lesson Plans

If you have surveyed this book, you noticed that it consists of lesson plans for the 48 major sound–symbol relationships in the English language. Each lesson plan includes three parts. The first part tells you how to *introduce* the sound. A specific, creative way to help children develop the sound–symbol relationship is described. You will also find a page of objects having that sound and a picture in which objects are hidden for each of the 48 sound–symbol relationships.

The second part of each lesson plan is for *reinforcement*. Children need many exposures to a sound in order to develop the association with the letter or letters that represent it. A reinforcement game or activity is provided in ready-to-use form for each of the 48 sound–symbol relationships.

The final part of each lesson plan, "Working with Words," emphasizes sound–symbol relationship using hands-on, multilevel activities. In this section you will use common phonograms to help students improve their reading and writing while reinforcing the sound being emphasized. Students will manipulate the most common phonograms with many consonants to create specific words. Let's take a closer look at each section.

Introducing the Sounds

The first part of the plan presents a way to introduce the sound to the children. As you glance through the introductions to various sounds, you will notice that a variety of activities are suggested for introducing the sounds. The association of a sound with a symbol requires that the child be attentive. Attention-getting introductions have been included so the child can see and hear the sound and symbol and begin making the association. If you like, you can mix and match the introductions to the various sounds. If, for example, your children prefer introductions with riddles, use them more frequently than indicated in the lesson plans.

In all of the introductions, you are actually writing words for the children to see. The written words emphasizing the letter the children are to associate with a particular sound are a very important part of the introduction. The children must do more than simply *hear* the sound—they should *see* the symbol that represents it. You may want to use colored chalk to highlight the letter they will associate with a particular sound.

After you have introduced the sound and the letter(s) that represents it, give the children the list of the hidden objects. You have permission to duplicate a copy for each child in your classroom. Some teachers like to make a copy for use on the overhead projector, and this is permissible too.

You will find five to twelve "hidden" objects with the sound that is being emphasized. Although most of the objects will be familiar to the children, in some cases a word may be new. This gives you an opportunity to expand the vocabularies of your students.

In addition to looking at the pictures and at the words that precede each picture, have children trace the letter or symbol that represents the sound being taught. For example, in the list with the objects that begin with /b/, you should have the children trace the letter *b* in each word. Have them trace *only* the *b*, not the entire word. Remember, you are trying to help them make a particular sound–symbol association. As they trace the letter, encourage them to say the sound and/or the word.

When the children are aware of the objects and have said the name of each one, give each child a copy of the hidden picture to find the objects. According to our field-testing results, most of the objects can be found within three minutes. To make the child successful, some objects are obvious. Other objects require more searching. As the children find the hidden objects, have them mention what they have found so that they are again saying the sound.

Make sure you summarize each lesson by writing the letter on the board and asking the children what sound they will say when they see that letter. Provide for the transfer of learning by having the children find words with that sound in their reading materials. You may want to keep a list of the words that you or the children use throughout the day that contain the sound. These can be read at the end of the day and used to strengthen the sound–symbol relationship.

In addition to using the list of hidden objects to have the children hear the sound being taught, you might want to have them make a scrapbook of the sounds they are learning. This is possible if you duplicate an additional copy of the hidden-objects list for each child. You might want the children to cut apart the pictures of the hidden objects and mix them up with other pictures or words. The children can then separate them by sounds if you provide a baggie or container for each sound.

The hidden pictures can be used in a variety of ways. Since many of the pictures deal with common childhood experiences, you may want to develop some language-experience selections that can also be used to help the children learn to read. Begin the language-experience activity by talking with the children about experiences of their own that are like those in the picture. After the children have shared their experiences, tell them that they would make a good story. Ask them how to begin the story. Write it down as the children dictate. Accept their language even when the grammar is incorrect; later you can teach them the correct way of expressing certain ideas.

Once you have developed the selection—be it a couple of sentences or a story—you can duplicate it and have the children read what they have dictated. Then use the selection to help them learn the sound. The children can go back through the words in the selection to find words that have the sound being emphasized.

The children may enjoy coloring some pictures. You may want to make a bulletin board of hidden pictures to serve as a review of the sounds. You can work on comprehension skills by having the children suggest titles for the pictures. Of course, many parents will enjoy watching their children find the objects in the picture, and this can serve as a review. Children of all ages seem to enjoy finding hidden objects in pictures; for children with learning disabilities, the opportunity to distinguish figure-ground relationships is especially valuable.

The hidden pictures can be useful as ten-minute time fillers and at the same time provide you with an opportunity for review and reinforcement. You may want to laminate some of the pictures and have them available at learning centers. The pictures can be self-correcting if you duplicate a copy of the hidden picture and color the hidden objects so they are obvious to the children.

Reinforcing the Sounds

All teachers are aware of the fact that children need practice to reinforce the association between sounds and symbols. A game or activity is provided for each of the 48 sound–symbol relationships in this book. The directions for introducing the activities are found in the second part of each lesson plan. You have permission to duplicate copies for all the children so they can use them for future reinforcement. You may want to color and laminate a copy of an activity for extension use at a learning center. The game boards are ready to use except for dice, tokens, or spinners. For some activities you will be asked to attach a spinner to the game board. This can easily be done by attaching a paper clip with a brad.

The size of each reinforcement game or activity is limited to 8½ × 11 inches; however, if you like, you can make the game board larger, so several children can use it at once. Make an overhead transparency, and then trace the activity on a large piece of cardboard or posterboard.

Children can do most of the reinforcement activities independently after you introduce them. There are a few activities you many want to use several times before children use them independently. It is important to use the activities with the children to make sure they are able to read the words that include the sound–symbol relationship. If you do keep laminated copies at a learning center, you might provide the answers on the back of the activity. Continually check to see whether the children are making the associations.

School volunteers, whether middle school students or grandparents, can also use the reinforcement activities in this book. You might assign one or more of your volunteers to use the pictures and activities with the children. The volunteers can even introduce the sound themselves, since the directions are detailed and any appropriate words are provided. School volunteers and aides can also help you prepare the materials, in addition to actually using them with children.

You may want to duplicate extra copies of the pictures and activities for children to take home. Parents can use the hidden pictures and reinforcement activities to review sounds that you have introduced.

Working with Words

The "Working with Words" activities are designed to help students learn the grapheme–phoneme relationship and recognize the most common word families in order to increase their proficiency in reading, spelling, and writing. In each "Working with Words" activity, students are actively involved by manipulating common phonograms or word families (Fry, 1998) to spell and recognize the most frequently appearing patterns in words (see Table 1 for list of phonograms). For example, in the lesson introducing /b/, students manipulate the consonant *b* and the letters of the common phonograms to make words such as *bay*, *bill*, *bat*, *bag* and *bell*. Fry (1998) reports that when adding beginning consonants to the 38 most common phonograms, students can create more than 650 different one-syllable words. Each of our lesson plans include "Working with Words" activities to use with your students. We included the most common phonograms and all possible words except those that elementary students do not use frequently, such as *cam*, or those that may be offensive. Remember, when selecting words for your activity, you must choose those that the child already has in his or her oral vocabulary.

Table 1

Most Common Phonograms in Rank Order
Based on Frequency
(Number of Uses in Monosyllabic Words)

Frequency	Phonogram	Example Words
26	-ay	jay say pay day play
26	-ill	hill bill will fill spill
22	-ip	ship dip tip skip trip
19	-at	cat fat bat rat sat
19	-am	ham jam Pam ram Sam
19	-ag	bag rag tag wag sag
19	-ack	back sack jack black track
19	-ank	bank sank tank bland brand
19	-ick	sick Dick pick quick chick
18	-ell	bell sell fell tell yell
18	-ot	pot not hot dot got
18	-ing	ring sing king wing thing
18	-ap	cap map tap clap trap
18	-unk	sunk junk bunk flunk skunk
17	-ail	pail jail nail sail tail
17	-ain	rain pain main chain plain
17	-eed	feed seed weed need freed
17	-y	my by dry try fly
17	-out	pout trout scout shout spout
17	-ug	rug bug hug dug tug
16	-op	mop cop pop top hop
16	-in	pin tin win chin thin
16	-an	pan man ran tan Dan
16	-est	best nest pest rest test
16	-ink	pink sink rink link drink
16	-ow	low slow grow show snow
16	-ew	new few chew grew blew
16	-ore	more sore tore store score
15	-ed	bed red fed led Ted
15	-ab	cab dab jab lab crab
15	-ob	cob job rob Bob knob

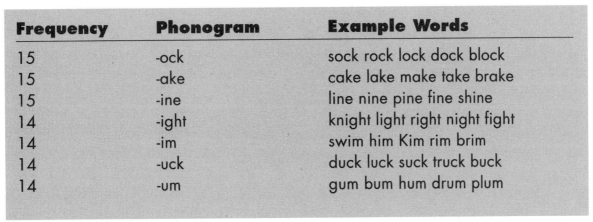

Frequency	Phonogram	Example Words
15	-ock	sock rock lock dock block
15	-ake	cake lake make take brake
15	-ine	line nine pine fine shine
14	-ight	knight light right night fight
14	-im	swim him Kim rim brim
14	-uck	duck luck suck truck buck
14	-um	gum bum hum drum plum

Source: Fry, 1998. Used with permission.

There are two related components in each of our "Working with Words" activities: word building and the transfer of spoken to written language. These components are related because children must make the connection that using phonograms to build words in these activities will help them when they need to decode or spell words during their independent reading. Word building provides students with both visual and auditory recognition of the target sound and phonograms and helps them develop the grapheme–phoneme relationship.

The transfer of spoken to written language enables students to write the words they just created and provides a connection between seeing and hearing the words and writing them. In order for the transfer of spoken to written language to be meaningful for children, they need to practice transferring their new skills to other situations. Using the example of /b/ mentioned above, you might ask students what common phonogram (e.g., -ay, -ill, -at, -ag, or -ell) would help them if they needed to spell the word *pill*. Students would then write this new word in their "Working with Words" notebook. As mentioned previously, students learn best when they write the words as well as see and hear them. Each child should maintain a notebook to write the words either individually or in sentences that they created during the "Working with Words" activity. The notebook can be created by stapling lined paper inside a construction-paper cover or by having each student bring in a spiral-type notebook. See page 15 for a sample format to use for your notebooks.

Working with Words Notebook

Words I learned today

1.

2.

3.

4.

5.

Word families I learned today

1.

2.

3.

4.

5.

Words I learned in sentences

1.

2.

3.

4.

5.

Before implementing the "Working with Words" activities with your students, prepare word cards with the alphabet letters used to represent the 38 most common phonograms as well as all consonants. There are several ways to prepare the word cards for students' use in the classroom. First, you can duplicate the letter and phonogram cards from Appendix B and prepare an individual set of cards for each student to keep in his or her desk. Each student needs four cards of each vowel, two of each consonant, and one of each phonogram. You may want to use two different colors of paper for the consonants and vowels, or underline the vowels to help children easily recognize the vowels. Laminate and cut out the cards and place them in individual Ziploc™ bags for easy storage. When it is time for a "Working with Words" activity, instruct students to take out their cards and select the phonograms and consonants used in the lesson.

A second method for preparing the word cards is to duplicate and laminate enough letters for a class set. Place the set in trays or boxes in an accessible classroom location. When it is time for the "Working with Words" activity, one student from each cooperative seating group selects the number of needed letters and distributes them to the students. (At the end of the activity, this student should collect the letters and return them to the tray.)

Two other techniques for preparing the word cards are to create large sandwich-type letters with yarn, which students can wear, or simply to use paper and pencil. When using the sandwich-type letters, several students can wear the letters and position themselves to spell the word with the represented sound such as /b/. If students are not comfortable wearing the word cards, they can hold them in front of their bodies. Using paper and pencil requires students to write the consonant followed by the common phonogram to spell each word in their "Working with Words" notebook.

Before implementing the activity, you also need to prepare larger word cards for teacher and class use. Using 3½ × 5-inch or similar index cards, write one letter on each card: four of each vowel and two of each consonant. Write vowels in red and the consonants in blue or black ink to help students differentiate vowels and consonants. During each "Working with Words" activity, students spell the word at their desks, and then one student spells the word aloud and then spells the word using the index card letters and a pocket chart.

Here are some key points to remember when teaching a "Working with Words" activity:

- Prepare the word cards ahead of time using volunteers or students to help you with the initial preparation.

- In each activity, you do not have to use all phonograms. Select a manageable number of phonograms, perhaps five to seven, to use in your lesson. If the target sound, such as /b/, can be used with numerous phonograms, use the "Working with Words" activity several times.

- Remember to say the target word aloud as well as use it in a sentence as students manipulate the phonograms and consonant(s). It is essential to emphasize the meaning of the words.

- After a student spells the word aloud, have him or her spell it using the index cards and the pocket chart or chalkboard ledge.

- Instruct students to manipulate the word cards on their desk or a table during "Working with Words."

- After a student spells the word aloud, he or she comes to the pocket chart and spells the word with the large letters for the class to view and self-correct the answers.

- Each "Working with Words" activity requires 15 to 30 minutes.

Now that you have the idea of "Working with Words," let's get started with a sample scripted lesson!

"Working with Words" Sample Scripted Lesson for /b/

Sound: /b/
Words: bay, bill, bat, bag, back, bank, bell, bunk, bail, by, bug, bin, best, bed, bake, bum, ban, bow, Bob, buck

Sound: /br/
Words: brag, bring, brew, brake

Sound: /bl/
Words: black, bleed, blink, blow, block

Instruct students to select their letters for this activity using one of the described procedures. We are only going to focus on the sound /b/, so students need the consonant *b* as well as the letters *a, b, e, g, i, l, t, u,* and *y*. Tell students they are starting a fun activity called "Working with Words" for each sound they learn (**T:** = Teacher's script).

T: Each time we learn a sound, we are going to practice that sound by using an activity called "Working with Words." I think you will like this activity because it is a fun way to learn the sounds of the letters and word families.

Tell students to place the letters on their desks in alphabetical order, write the consonant and vowels on the board, or place them in the pocket chart.

T: I would like you to put the letters on your desk in alphabetical order as you put them in the pocket chart.

Say aloud the sound of the consonant *b*, /b/, and read each letter as you point to them on the board.

T: Let's say the sound the letter *b* makes, /b/. You will hear /b/ in all of the words we make today. Let's also name each one of the letters *a*, *b*, *e*, *g*, *i*, *l*, *t*, *u*, and *y*. Great job everyone! Let's start making some words.

Begin by providing the students a prompt, such as, "Our first word has three letters, one vowel, and two consonants." Using one word at a time, tell students to move the letters from the top of their desks to spell the word. Say the word aloud and use the word in a sentence. After students have time to make the word, look around the classroom and call a student with the correct answer to say and spell the word aloud. When repeating the correct spelling of the word, point out the phonogram. Ask the child to come to the pocket chart and spell the word using the large letters on the index cards.

T: **Our first word has three letters, one vowel and two consonants. Place the letter** *b* **in front of you on your desk. I would like you to find the letters of the word family or phonogram** *-ay* (you may want to point to them in the pocket chart) **and move them next to the consonant** *b* **to spell the word** *bay*. **Some people like to fish in the** *bay*. **Great, I see** (insert child's name) **has this one correct. Please spell** *bay* **for us. Does everyone hear the /b/ sound? Let's say** *bay* **together.** *Bay*. (Child's

name), **please use the letters in the pocket chart to spell** *bay*. **If anyone did not spell** *bay* **correctly, change it now.**

T: **Our next word also has three letters. Keep the letter** *b* **and put the letters** *-ay* **back. Now find the letters to make the phonogram** *-ill* (you may want to point to them in the pocket chart). **Place the letters next to the letter** *b* **to spell the word** *bill*. **I have a one-dollar** *bill*. **Great, I see** (child's name) **has this one correct. Please spell** *bill* **for us. Does everyone hear the /b/ sound? Let's say** *bill* **together.** *Bill*. (Child's name), **please use the letters in the pocket chart to spell** *bill*. **If anyone did not spell** *bill* **correctly, change it now.**

T: **For our next word, keep the** *b*, **but put the letters** *-ill* **back. Find the letters of the phonogram** *-at* (you may want to point to them in the pocket chart). **Place them next to the letter** *b* **to spell the word** *bat*. **I hit the ball with a** *bat*. **Great, I see** (child's name) **has this one correct. Please spell** *bat* **for us. Does everyone hear the /b/ sound? Let's say** *bat* **together.** *Bat*. (Child's name), **please use the letters in the pocket chart to spell** *bat*. **If anyone did not spell** *bat* **correctly, change it now.**

T: **Put the letters of the word family or phonogram** *-at* **back and find the letters for the phonogram** *-ug* (you may want to point to them in the pocket chart). **Place them next to the letter** *b* **to spell the word** *bug*. **A** *bug* **sat on the rug. Great, I see** (child's name) **has this one correct. Please spell** *bug* **for us. Does everyone hear the /b/ sound? Let's say** *bug* **together.** *Bug*. (Child's name), **please use the letters in the** pocket chart to spell *bug*. If anyone did not spell *bug* correctly, change it now.

T: Our next word has three letters starting with the letter *b* and ending with the letter *g*. Put the letters of the word family -*ug* back and find the letters for the phonogram -*ag* (you may want to point to them in the pocket chart). **Place them next to the letter *b* to spell the word *bag*. We carried our groceries in a *bag*. Great, I see** (insert child's name) **has this one correct. Please spell *bag* for us. Does everyone hear the /b/ sound? Let's say *bag* together. *Bag*.** (Child's name), **please use the letters in the pocket chart to spell *bag*. If anyone did not spell *bag* correctly, change it now.**

T: Our last word of the day also has three letters. Put the word family or phonogram -*ag* back and find the letters for the phonogram -*ell* (you may want to point to them in the pocket chart). **Place them next to the letter *b* to spell the word *bell*. The school *bell* rings at eight o'clock. Great, I see** (child's name) **has this one correct. Please spell *bell* for us. Does everyone hear the /b/ sound? Let's say *bell* together. *Bell*.** (Child's name), **please use the letters in the pocket chart to spell *bell*. If anyone did not spell *bell* correctly, change it now.**

Now you have used all of the target phonograms to create words with the sound /b/ in this activity. Instruct students to take out their "Working with Words" notebooks and write down the words they created during the lesson.

Next, have students write each word in an original sentence.

T: **Class, everyone did a great job with this activity today. Let's take out our "Working with Words" notebooks and write down the words you created today. As you write each word, remember to say each word to yourself and listen for the /b/ sound. If I wanted to spell the word *day*, what word family that we used today could help me? Right, -*ay*. Write this word in your notebook. After you write the words, use each one in a sentence.**

During another "Working with Words" activity, you can use additional phonograms to reinforce /b/ or introduce a blend such as /bl/ or /br/.

The same format from this scripted lesson is used in each "Working with Words" activity in this book. The letters of common phonograms are used repeatedly with each sound to create meaningful words. The number of phonograms used in each activity varies depending on the number of words that are created. Some activities, such as the /b/ activity, contain more phonograms than the activity for the sound /g/. Remember, choose the number of phonograms that works best for you and your students. Finally, continue to emphasize the meanings of the words by using them in sentences.

If you would like a paraprofessional or volunteer in your classroom to use the activity with a small group of students, they can complete and follow the blank script in Appendix A.

Sounds in the English Language

The English language is a difficult one to learn to read, because although there are 45 sounds, the alphabet contains only 26 letters. Twenty-four sounds are consonant sounds and 21 are vowel sounds. Tables 3 and 4 show key words for the 24 consonant sounds and the 21 vowel sounds. Table 5 shows some of the common *consonant blends* (a consonant sound that is produced by blending two consonants into one sound). Examine the chart with the consonant sounds and the chart with the vowel sounds to familiarize yourself with the 45 sounds.

As you look at the chart of consonant sounds, you will notice that most consonant sounds are represented by one letter; however, some of these sounds consist of two letters that make one sound: *ch*, *ng*, *sh*, *th*, and *wh*. These consonant combinations are called *consonant digraphs* because the two letters produce a *new* sound that is not like the blend of the sounds of the two component letters. Consonant digraphs and consonant blends are alike in that they are both made up of two or three letters representing one sound; they are different in that consonant blends are not new or distinctive sounds, but rather a blend of two existing sounds into one sound, while consonant digraphs are entirely new sounds.

As you examine the chart of the consonant sounds, you will see three letters in the alphabet that do not have distinctive sounds of their own. The letter *c* can equal /k/ or /s/. The letter *c*
does not have its own sound. Likewise, the letter *q* is /kw/ or /k/, but does not have its own sound. The letter *x* can represent three different sounds (/ks/, /z/, or /gz/), none of which is its own. Lesson plans are provided for *c*, *q*, and *x* so children can learn what sounds these letters represent. Thus, there are 48 rather than 45 lessons in this book.

Now let us take a closer look at the chart of the vowel sounds. In general, five letters—*a*, *e*, *i*, *o*, and *u*—are used to represent 21 different sounds. Of course, the letter *y* more often serves as a vowel than a consonant; however, *y* does not have a distinctive vowel sound. Generally *y* sounds like long *i*, long *e*, short *i*, or short *e*. In some reading series, *w*, *r*, and *l* are considered semivowels since they can follow *a*, *e*, *i*, *o*, or *u* to represent a particular vowel sound.

Notice that each vowel letter has a long-vowel sound like its name: "Apes eat ice over Utah." Each vowel letter also has a short sound: "Fat Ed is not up." In addition to the long- and short-vowel sounds, new vowels are formed when the letter *r* follows a vowel letter, as in "Are bears near her door?" when the letters *l*, *u*, and *w* follow *a*, the broad *a* sound (as in *ball*, *haul*, and *law*) is likely to occur.

Two of the vowel sounds are called *diphthongs*. A diphthong is produced by two different vowels that glide together to produce one sound. The diphthongs in English are *oi* or *oy* as in *oil* and *boy*, and *ou* or *ow* as in *mouth* and *cow*. When two *o*s appear together, they do not produce a diphthong but rather a new sound. The sound of the long double *o* is /oo/, as in *tool*. Short double *o* sounds like /oo/, as in *book*.

The final vowel sound is the *schwa* sound. The schwa sound is defined as the vowel sound in unaccented syllables. All vowel letters can represent the schwa sound, as in *ago, telegram, helicopter, official,* and *focus*. The schwa sounds a little like a short *u*; however, it is not as easily distinguishable, since it is in the unaccented syllable. Here is a sentence containing the schwa, broad *a*, diphthong, and double *o* sounds: "Balloons cause boys to look out."

As you look at the vowel chart, you will notice *diacritical markings* over some of the vowels. The diacritical markings are used to indicate the sounds that each vowel represents. Remember that diacritical markings vary from dictionary to dictionary and from reading series to reading series. Be sure to use the diacritical markings that are found in your reading series, spelling book, textbook glossaries, or in the dictionaries available in your school. The diacritical markings used in this book commonly appear in material for elementary schoolchildren.

Since there is disagreement concerning the number of sounds in English, it will be necessary for you to select the lesson plans that correspond to the sounds you teach as part of your reading program. You are the expert on your children, so teach them the sounds they normally speak. Likewise, there is no magical sequence in which children learn the different sounds. Table 2 can be used as a guide if you need a suggested order for teaching the sounds.

Table 2

Sequence of Phonics Instruction

Teach These Sounds First

/b/, /ă/, /t/, /ĕ/, /m/, /s/, /n/, /r/, /d/, /ĭ/, /p/, /ŏ/

Teach These Sounds Next

/ē/, /ō/, /l/, /f/, /k/, /ā/, /ī/, /ū/ /w/, c = /k/, /h/, /g/

Teach These Sounds Now

/th/, /ẽr/, /sh/, /ng/, c = /s/, /ch/, /ôr/, /är/, /v/, /â/, /ū/, /ou/

Work on These Last

/z/, /j/, /wh/, /à/, /y/, /ōō/, /êr/, /ŏŏ/, /oi/, q = /kw/, schwa, x = /ks/, /gz/, or /z/

Table 3

Consonant Sounds

b	c = /k/	c = /s/
ball	cat	circle
ch	d	f
chain	dog	foot
g	h	j
ghost	hat	jeep
k	l	m
key	ladder	monkey
n	ng	p
nest	ring	pig
q	r	s
queen	rope	sun
sh	t	*th* and th
shark	turtle	feather, thumb
v	w	wh
vase	wagon	wheel
x	y	z
X ray	yo-yo	zebra

Table 4

Vowel Sounds

ā	ă	är
cake	apple	star
âr	à	ē
chair	ball	tree
ě	ẽr	êr
egg	bird	ear
ī	ĭ	ō
kite	fish	bone
ǒ	o͞o	o͝o
octopus	spoon	book
ou, ow	oi	ôr
owl	oil	fork
ŭ	ū	ə
truck	unicycle	banana

Table 5

Selected Consonant Blends

bl	br	cl	cr	dr
blouse	broom	clown	crayon	drum
fl	fr	gl	gr	pl
flag	frog	gloves	grapes	plug
pr	sc, sch, sk	sm	sn	sp
pretzel	scooter	smoke	snake	spear
st	sw	scr	spl	tr
star	seing	screw	splinter	tree
thr	spr	squ	str	tw
three	spring	squirrel	strawberry	tweezers

Assessing Children's Knowledge of Phonics

Since the children, not the phonics curriculum, should be the major consideration in determining what particular sound/symbol relationships to teach, it is necessary to assess the needs of the children. Often you will know what sound/symbol relationships to teach because of observations you have made. For example, if a child is reading and comes to an unfamiliar word, you should ask what part of the word is difficult and, when he points to a particular symbol or pattern, ask him what sound it represents. If the child does not know, you have identified an objective.

Analyzing misspelled words on a spelling test can also help you determine objectives. If a child spells *bird* by writing *brid*, you know that she does not understand the *br* blend or the fact that *ir* represents /er/. Observation can be one of your best assessment devices if you are aware of the many aspects of phonics.

If you need informal tests to determine the particular sound/symbol relationships and generalizations a child should learn, we have provided five individually administered tests in this book:

Test A:	Easier Sounds
Test B:	More Difficult Sounds
Test C:	Consonant Blends
Test D:	Most Frequent Sound Patterns
Test E:	More Sound Patterns

We've provided individual rather than group tests because many group tests are already available, and because the results from an individual test in which the child actually pronounces the word are more valid than the results of a group test.

Notice that copies of the test words are provided for the students, and separate teacher worksheets are provided for you. Remove the teacher worksheets from the book and duplicate the number of copies you need. Write the child's name and date on the teacher worksheet for the test you want to administer. The child will read the words on the student's copy as you follow along on the teacher worksheet. The administration of each test requires approximately three to five minutes.

Begin the testing situation by telling the child you have some words you would like her to pronounce. Say the words will look new or silly because they may be "nonsense words." Encourage the child to sound out each word. When administering Test C, tell the child that all the words end in *at*. Remind the child you are going to be taking some notes about what sounds to teach. Begin administering the test of your choice and administer as many tests as you desire while you have the child's attention. Stop administering the tests when you have identified a few sounds to teach.

As the child reads the words from the student's copy, follow along on the appropriate teacher worksheet. If the child says the word correctly, put a plus (+) in the blank after the word. If the child does not try to sound out the word, write D.T. (didn't try) in the blank. If the child sounds out the word incorrectly, write down exactly what she said so you can determine what particular sounds or principles she is confusing or does not know. Notice the following example:

Teacher Worksheet

Student's Name: _Yolanda Mott_

Date: _9/25/00_

Test A: Easier Sounds

Test Words	Correct Pronunciation	Child's Response	Corresponding Lesson Plan
1. bab	bab	+	/b/
2. dod	dod	+	/d/
3. mim	mim	+	/m/
4. nin	nin	+	/n/
5. pip	pip	D.T.	/p/
6. rab	rab	tab	/r/
7. ses	ses	+	/s/

After you have completed the administration of a test, notice the errors the child has made. For example, if a child has pronounced *pap* for *bab*, it may be because she cannot visually discriminate *b* and *p*. If the child pronounces *ket* for *cet*, she does not know the fact that c represents /s/ when followed by *e*. Keep in mind that you are testing the child's knowledge of the sound represented by the italicized letters of the test word, but that at the same time you can make observations about other aspects of phonics. For example, if the child says *babe* for *bab*, she did pronounce the sound of *b* correctly in both the initial and final positions, and this is what you are testing when you ask a child to read the first word in Test A. At the same time you realize the child is not able to apply the closed-syllable principle or the final silent *e* principle, and you will want to make a note of this. Space is provided at the bottom of each teacher worksheet for observations about the child.

Student's Copy of Words
(Tests A, B, and C)

Test A	Test B	Test C
1. bab	1. cem	1. blat
2. dod	2. charch	2. brat
3. mim	3. tong	3. clat
4. nin	4. sharsh	4. crat
5. pip	5. tharth	5. drat
6. rab	6. vav	6. dwat
7. ses	7. lu	7. flat
8. tat	8. gar	8. frat
9. ab	9. gare	9. glat
10. eb	10. ler	10. grat
11. ib	11. lor	11. plat
12. ob	12. fouth	12. prat
13. ub	13. jat	13. scat
14. cam	14. quat	14. slat
15. gog	15. whap	15. smat
16. hab	16. ux	16. snat
17. kak	17. yab	17. spat
18. lell	18. zaz	18. stat
19. fam	19. lear	19. strat
20. wab	20. naul	20. skat
21. tabe	21. pook	21. shrat
22. ke	22. doon	22. thrat
23. bi	23. doy	23. trat
24. fo	24. ahang	24. shrat

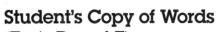

Student's Copy of Words
(Tests D and E)

Directions: Some letters are together. Say the sound of each set of letters.

	Test D			**Test E**	
1.	ay		1.	ab	
2.	ill		2.	ob	
3.	ip		3.	et	
4.	at		4.	ock	
5.	am		5.	ace	
6.	ag		6.	ake	
7.	ack		7.	um	
8.	ank		8.	ad	
9.	ick		9.	ight	
10.	ell		10.	un	
11.	ot		11.	ame	
12.	ing		12.	ade	
13.	ap		13.	ate	
14.	unk		14.	unch	
15.	ail		15.	ung	
16.	ain		16.	ine	
17.	eed		17.	ide	
18.	out		18.	im	
19.	ug		19.	ut	
20.	op		20.	ew	
21.	in		21.	ust	
22.	an		22.	uck	
23.	est		23.	aw	
24.	ink		24.	ump	
25.	ore		25.	ed	

Teacher Worksheet A

Student's Name: _____

Date: _____

Test A: Easier Sounds

Test Words	Correct Pronunciation	Child's Response	Corresponding Lesson Plan (circle needs)
1. bab	băb		/b/
2. dod	dŏd		/d/
3. mim	mĭm		/m/
4. nin	nĭn		/n/
5. pip	pĭp		/p/
6. rab	răb		/r/
7. ses	sĕs		/s/
8. tat	tăt		/t/
9. ab	ăb		/ă/
10. eb	ĕb		/ĕ/
11. ib	ĭb		/ĭ/
12. ob	ŏb		/ŏ/
13. ub	ŭb		/ŭ/
14. cam	kăm		c = /k/
15. gog	gŏg		/g/
16. hab	hăb		/h/
17. kak	kăk		/k/
18. lell	lĕl		/l/
19. fam	făm		/f/
20. wab	wăb		/w/
21. tabe	tāb		/ā/
22. ke	kē		/ē/
23. bi	bī		/ī/
24. bo	bō		/ō/

Teacher Worksheet B

Student's Name: _____

Date: _____

Test B: More Difficult Sounds

Test Words	Correct Pronunciation	Child's Response	Corresponding Lesson Plan (circle needs)
1. cem	sĕm		c = /s/
2. charch	chärch		/ch/
3. tong	tŏng		/ng/
4. sharsh	shärsh		/sh/
5. tharth	thärth		/th/
6. vav	văv		/v/
7. lu	lū		/ū/
8. gar	gär		/är/
9. gare	gâre		/â/
10. ler	lẽr		/ẽr/
11. lor	lôr		/ôr/
12. fouth	fouth		/ou/
13. jat	jăt		/j/
14. quat	kwăt		q = /kw/
15. whap	hwăp		/wh/
16. ux	ŭks		x = /eks/
17. yab	yăb		/y/
18. zaz	zăz		/z/
19. lear	lêr		/ê/
20. naul	nȧul		/ȧ/
21. pook	pŏok		/ŏo/
22. doon	dōon		/ōo/
23. doy	doy		/oi/
24. ahang	a/hang		ə

Teacher Worksheet C

Student's Name: _____

Date: _____

Test C: Consonant Blends

Test Words	Correct Pronunciation	Child's Response	Corresponding Lesson Plan (circle needs)
1. blat	blăt		b
2. brat	brăt		b
3. clat	clăt		c = /k/
4. crat	crăt		c = /k/
5. drat	drăt		d
6. dwat	dwăt		d
7. flat	flăt		f
8. frat	frăt		f
9. glat	glăt		g
10. grat	grăt		g
11. plat	plăt		p
12. prat	prăt		p
13. scat	scăt		s
14. slat	slăt		s
15. smat	smăt		s
16. snat	snăt		s
17. spat	spăt		s
18. stat	stăt		s
19. strat	străt		s
20. skat	skăt		s
21. shrat	shrăt		s
22. thrat	thrăt		th
23. trat	trăt		t

Teacher Worksheet D

Student's Name: _____

Date: _____

Test D: Most Frequent Sound Patterns

Test Words	Correct Pronunciation		Child's Response	Corresponding Lesson Plan (circle needs)
1. ay	ā	as in day		/ā/
2. ill	ĭll	as in till		/ĭ/
3. ip	ĭp	as in dip		/ĭ/
4. at	ăt	as in cat		/ă/
5. am	ăm	as in ham		/ă/
6. ag	ăg	as in bag		/ă/
7. ack	ăck	as in back		/ă/
8. ank	ănk	as in bank		/ă/
9. ick	ĭck	as in lick		/ĭ/
10. ell	ĕll	as in sell		/ĕ/
11. ot	ŏt	as in not		/ŏ/
12. ing	ĭng	as in sing		/ĭ/
13. ap	ăp	as in map		/ă/
14. unk	ŭnk	as in dunk		/ŭ/
15. ail	āil	as in mail		/ā/
16. ain	āin	as in rain		/ā/
17. eed	sēe	as in seed		/ē/
18. out	out	as in shout		/ou/
19. ug	ŭg	as in bug		/ŭ/
20. op	ŏp	as in top		/ŏ/
21. in	in	as in fin		/ĭ/
22. an	an	as in can		/ă/
23. est	est	as in best		/ĕ/
24. ink	ink	as in sink		/ĭ/
25. ore	ore	as in store		/ôr/

Teacher Worksheet E

Student's Name: _____

Date: _____

Test E: More Sound Patterns

Test Words	Correct Pronunciation		Child's Response	Corresponding Lesson Plan (circle needs)
1. ab	ăb	as in cab		/ă/
2. ob	ŏb	as in job		/ŏ/
3. et	ĕt	as in jet		/ĕ/
4. ock	ŏck	as in sock		/ŏ/
5. ace	āc	as in face		/ā/
6. ake	āk	as in cake		/ā/
7. um	ŭm	as in gum		/ŭ/
8. ad	ăd	as in bad		/ă/
9. ight	īt	as in light		/ī/
10. un	ŭn	as in bun		/ŭ/
11. ame	ām	as in game		/ā/
12. ade	ād	as in made		/ā/
13. ate	āt	as in date		/ā/
14. unch	ŭnch	as in lunch		/ŭ/
15. ung	ŭng	as in hung		/ŭ/
16. ine	īn	as in line		/ī/
17. ide	īd	as in tide		/ī/
18. im	ĭm	as in him		/ĭ/
19. ut	ŭt	as in but		/ŭ/
20. ew	ew	as in new		/ū/
21. ust	ŭst	as in dust		/ŭ/
22. uck	ŭck	as in duck		/ŭ/
23. aw	ȧw	as in law		/ȧ/
24. ump	ŭmp	as in jump		/ŭ/
25. ed	ĕd	as in bed		/ĕ/

PART II

Lesson Plans, Pictures, and Activities

ă

as in apple

Introducing /ă/

1. Begin this lesson by writing the following words on the board:

apple	that	as	can
have	had	man	an
after	has	and	bat

2. Ask the children to be spies and see whether they can find out how all of these words are alike. If they know these words by sight, you might have the children read them aloud to hear how they are alike. If not, you can read them for the children.

3. After the children have observed the letter *a* in each word (or perhaps

/ă/), you can tell them that the letter *a* is one of the vowels. If this is their first introduction to vowels, define a vowel by saying that the letters *a, e, i, o, u,* and sometimes *y* are vowels. Tell the children that all words have vowels. You might explain that vowel letters make many *different* sounds.

4. Tell them the vowel letter *a* can make six sounds. You will teach them the short sound first. Say, "Short *a* sounds like /ă/, as in *apple*." Have the children say "apple" and then simply say "/ă/."

5. Read the words listed above and have the children repeat them, emphasizing the /ă/ sound. Now direct the children's attention to the list of the hidden objects. As they say each word, they should listen to hear the /ă/. Now have the children find the hidden objects and again review the short a sound.

Reinforcing /ă/

Tell children they will make many words with short a. Ask them to be workers in the word factory, and give them a copy of the reinforcement activity, "Word Factory." They will notice the small words *an*, *am*, and *at* at the top and bottom of the mixer. They are to find consonants that can be combined with one of these small words to make new words. For example, they may add *c* to *an* to make the word *can*. They would then write *can* on the line under the *an* column. Encourage the children to make as many words as they can. After the children have made words, have them read their words, use them in sentences, and again notice the short a sound.

Working with Words for /ă/

1. There are many frequently appearing sound patterns that have the short a sound. Use these words to help children learn the patterns.

ack

back	snack	lack
shack	crack	tack
sack	black	rack
snack	quack	pack
jack	smack	
track	stack	

ad

add	had	pad
bad	glad	sad
dad	mad	

ă

ag
bag   flag   rag
brag   gag   sag
drag   nag   snag
         wag   tag

am
dam   Pam   slam
swam   mam   jam
clam   ram   Sam
ham   tram

an
an   Jan   ran
can   tan   than
man   Dan   fan
plan   pan   Stan
              van

ank
bank   Frank   sank
blank   plank   spank
drank   prank   tank
         rank   thank

ap
cap   trap   snap
lap   gap   tap
map   pap   clap
nap   wrap   sap
rap   slap   strap

at
at   rat   hat
cat   that   pat
flat   bat   sat
mat   fat   chat

PATCH

2. Additional sound patterns you may wait to teach your students are:

ab

cab	tab	grab
gab	blab	scab
jab	crab	slab
lab	drab	stab
nab		

amp

camp	cramp	ramp
champ	damp	stamp
clamp	lamp	tramp

ance

chance	glance	stance
dance	prance	trance

and

band	brand	gland
hand	sand	stand
land		

ang

bang	gang	rang
clang	hang	sprang
fang		

ant

can't	Grant	plant
chant	pant	slant

ash

cash	hash	smash
dash	flash	trash
gash		

ast

cast	fast	past
blast	last	vast
	mast	

atch

batch	match	snatch
catch	patch	thatch
hatch		

Hidden Pictures

anchor
ant
apple
ax
basket
bat
hat
mask
paddle
pan

38

Name_____ Date_____

Word Factory

Directions: You can make words by finding letters to go with *an*, *ag*, and *at*. Find a letter to add to the beginning of *an*, *ag*, or *at* to make words like *tan*, *tag*, and *sat*. Write the new words you make under *an*, *ag*, or *at*. Use your new words in sentences.

an

1. _____
2. _____
3. _____
4. _____
5. _____

ag

1. _____
2. _____
3. _____
4. _____
5. _____

at

1. _____
2. _____
3. _____
4. _____
5. _____

ā

as in cake

Introducing /ā/

1. Divide the children into two teams to play "20 Questions." Ask each team a question. Tell them that all of the answers to the questions will be words that have the long *a* sound, as in *ate, pay, aid, rain, able,* and *late.* Remind them that the team with the most points is the winner.

2. Team members will take turns answering these questions.

1. What horses like to eat. (hay)

2. Prisoners must stay in _____. (jail)

3. You can hit it with a hammer. (nail)

4. A reward you get for working. (pay)

5. A bird that is blue. (bluejay)

6. What you use to catch fish. (bait)

7. What dogs wag when they are happy. (tail)

8. How old you are. (age)

9. What stores have when they lower the prices. (sale)

10. A purple fruit or drink. (grape)

11. All books have them. (pages)

12. To run after someone. (chase)

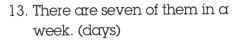

13. There are seven of them in a week. (days)

14. A small bucket. (pail)

15. The bread is not fresh, it is _____. (stale)

16. What I ask you to write on your papers. (name)

17. What the postman brings. (mail)

18. A place without sun. (shade)

19. At recess time you go out to ____. (play)

20. You can use it to make things stick. (paste)

As the children answer the questions, emphasize the long *a* sound as you write their answers on the board.

3. Now direct their attention to the list of hidden objects. Again have them notice /ā/, like the name of the letter *a*. Have them find the objects in the picture and again they will have the opportunity to say the long *a* sound.

Reinforcing /ā/

1. Show the children how to play "Skate or Wait." Hand out this reinforcement activity. Read the first two words, *mad* and *maid,* and ask the children to tell you the difference. Lead the children to see *ai* makes the long *a* sound and *a* between two consonants makes ā.

2. The players take turns spinning a spinner or throwing a die to see how many spaces they can move. To move the number of spaces on the spinner, the player must read the word on the space where he will land. If the child cannot, he moves back to the first word he can read other than *skate.* Players *skate* or *wait,* as directed on the game board.

3. Notice that all but the last path on the game board include words that have the /ā/ sound because of the *ai* combination. The last path includes words that have the long *a* sound because of a final, silent *e.* The children will learn the importance of looking at each letter or pattern in a word in order to read it correctly. Have the children notice the effect of *i* in the *ai* combination and of *e* in the silent *e* words. Tell them that when they see these patterns, they should try the long *a* sound.

Working with Words for /ā/

1. Use these words to help children notice frequently appearing phonograms.

ay

clay	gay	jay	play
hay	pay	ray	spray
may	gray	tray	sway
say	stay	day	way
stray	lay	bay	pray

ake

bake	brake	cake	fake
Jake	lake	make	rake
snake	stake	shake	take

ail

bail	fail	hail	jail
mail	nail	pail	rail
sail	snail	tail	trail

ain

brain	chain	drain	gain
main	plain	pain	rain
train	grain	stain	

2. Additional phonograms that you can teach children are:

ace

brace	lace	race
face	pace	space
grace	place	trace

ade

blade	grade	shade
fade	made	spade
		trade

age

cage page stage
rage wage

ale

bale gale sale
Dale male scale
pale tale

ame

blame flame name
came frame same
dame lame shame
fame tame

ane

cane lane plane
crane mane sane
Jane pane vane

ape

cape drape scrape
tape grape shape

ate

crate hate plate
date Kate rate
fate late skate
gate mate state

Hidden Pictures

cage
cake
cane
nail
paint
plate
snake
vase

Name_____ Date_____

Skate or Wait

Directions: Put a token on Start for each player. Spin a spinner to see how many spaces you can move. To move, you must read the word on the space on which you land. If you cannot read the word, you move back to the first word you can read. You miss a turn when you land on *Wait.* You move ahead if you land on *Skate.* The first one to land on the word *Win* is the winner!

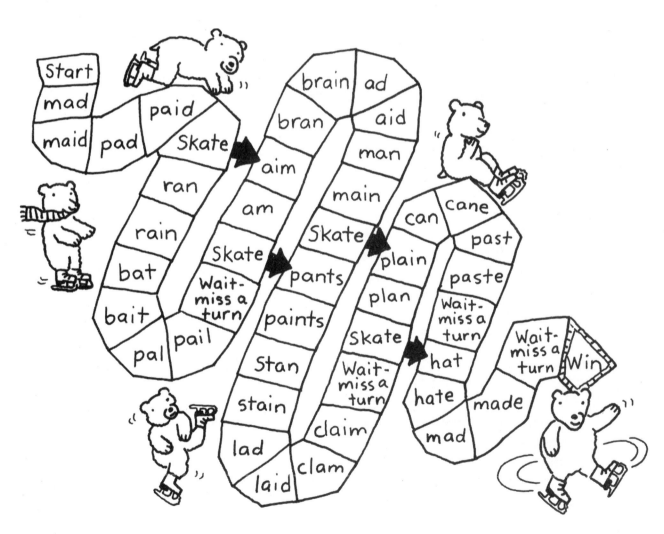

45

är

as in star

 ## Introducing /är/

1. Tell the children one letter of the alphabet is very bossy. When the vowels are in front of that letter, they must say a new sound—not a long or a short sound, but a *new* vowel sound. Tell them the bossy letter is *r*.

2. Write these words on the board: *bar, car, art, far, jar,* and *star.* Ask the children what vowel letter is in front of the letter *r*. Then have them listen as you say the words. Have them notice the /är/ sound. Now give them the opportunity to repeat the words after you, so they can say "/är/."

3. Sometimes when *a* and *r* are together, the sound you hear is like the name of the letter *r*. See if the children can think of any other words in which they hear /är/. If not, suggest such words as *dart, smart, starve, card, sharp, yard, are, large,* and *farm.*

4. Now have the children look at the list of the hidden objects. Have them trace the *ar* combinations as they say the words having /är/. The children can now have fun finding the objects hidden in the picture.

Reinforcing /är/

1. Hand out the reinforcement activity. Tell the children that when all of the letters of the alphabet play "King or Queen of the Mountain," the letter *r* is always on top because it is so bossy. In fact, the letter *r* will not allow any word on top of the mountain unless it has an *r* in it. Tell the children these words are trying to get up on top of the mountain, but cannot because they do not have an *r*.

2. Ask the children to write the letter *r* after the *a*, and then say the word that is trying to get on top of the mountain. If they are able to say that word, the letter *r* will let the word join it at the top so it can be a king or queen too. The children should then write their new words in the spaces provided so they have another opportunity to feel the /är/ combination.

Working with Words for /är/

1. Use these sound patterns to have children notice the words with /är/:

ar

bar	jar	tar
car	mar	scar
far	par	star

ard

card	hard	yard
guard	lard	

ark

bark	mark	spark
dark	park	stark
lark	shark	

art

cart	part	smart
dart	tart	start
mart	chart	

Hidden Pictures

arch
arm
car
card
dart
heart
jar
marble
star
target

Name_____ Date_____

King or Queen of the Mountain

Directions: In order to become king or queen of the mountain, these words need an *r*. Bossy *r* will not let any word on top unless it has an *r*. Add an *r* to each word and write the new words at the top. Use each new word in a sentence.

âr

as in chair

Introducing /âr/

1. Before you begin this lesson, make a simple paper airplane. Introduce the lesson by flying the airplane and asking the children to tell you what vowel sound they hear in the word *plane*. They should say /ā/. If not, you can stress /ā/ and have them hear the long *a* sound.

2. Now ask the children what sound they hear in the word *air*. They will say /â/. Tell them this is another vowel sound the letter *a* can make when it is in front of *r* followed by *e*, or in the *air* combination. Write the word *air* on the board and ask whether the children can make

other words by adding consonants or consonant combinations: *chair, fair, hair, pair.*

3. Now write the following words on the board: *bar, car, far, par,* and *star.* Add an *e* at the end of each of the words and then read them for the children. Use the words in sentences. Again, direct the children's attention to /â/.

4. Have children look at the list of the hidden objects and stress the /a/ as the children say the names of the objects. They should take a deep breath to get lots of *air,* and then as they find the objects, stress /â/.

Reinforcing /âr/

Give each student a copy of the reinforcement activity "We Need Air." Read the words in the word box with the students, highlighting the different spellings of the /âr/ sound. Students work individually or with a partner to use the words from the word box to complete the story. Each word can be used more than once. After completing the story, students can read their story aloud to a partner.

Working with Words for /âr/

Use these sound patterns to help teach children the sound /âr/:

air

air	hair	chair
fair	pair	stair

are

bare	hare	scare
care	mare	share
dare	rare	spare
fare	flare	square
	glare	stare

Hidden Pictures

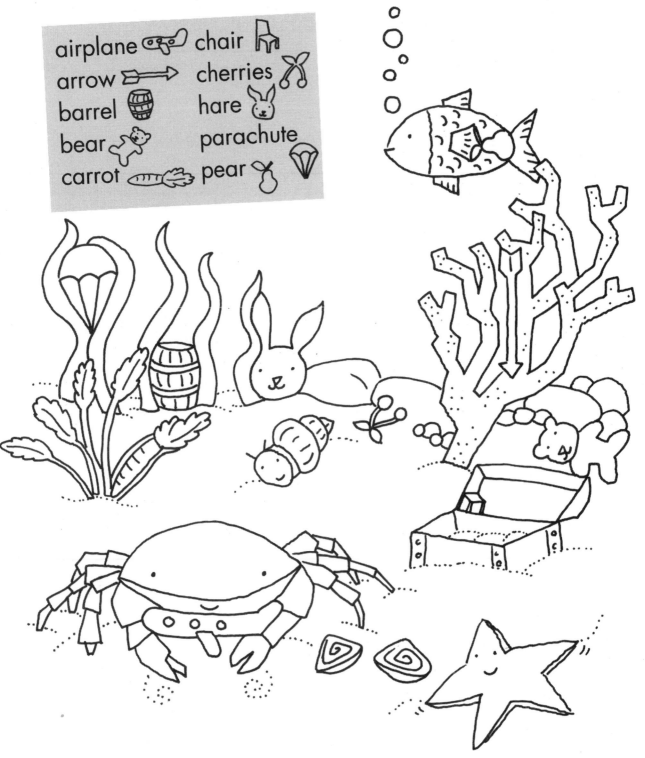

airplane
arrow
barrel
bear
carrot

chair
cherries
hare
parachute
pear

Name_____ Date_____

We Need Air

Directions: Use the following words to complete the story about air. Each word can be used more than one time. Remember to say each word as you write it.

air	where	declare	aware	hare	square
chair	bear	beware	careful	dictionary	

Are you aw__ __ __ that we need to breathe a __ __? I

d__ __ __ __ __ __ __ we must have a__ __. Does a h __ __ __

need a __ __? Of course a h __ __ __ needs a __ __! Does a

ch __ __ __ need a __ __? NO! Does a b __ __ __ need a __ __?

Yes! Does a sq __ __ __ __ need a __ __? NO. Only living things

need a __ __. Wh __ __ __ do we get a __ __? Look it up in the

d __ __ __ __ __ __ __ __ __ __. Be __ __ __ __! You are in trouble

if you don't have a __ __. Now you should be aw __ __ __ you

have to breathe a __ __, so be c __ __ __ __ __ __ __!

ȧ
as in *ball*

Introducing /ȧ/

1. Begin this lesson by doing a dance. Say "*cha-cha-cha*" as you move your feet. Have the children stand and try the dance as they say "*cha-cha-cha.*"

2. After the children are seated, ask them what consonant sound they heard at the beginning of *cha*. Now ask them the vowel sound. See if they can think of any other words that have /ȧ/. If they are not able to think of others, you can suggest these:

al/all	aw	au
tall	draw	cause
hall	jaw	pause
call	raw	haul
talk	saw	fault
walk	crawl	maul
salt	awful	clause

3. Tell the children that sometimes when *a* is in front of *l*, *w*, or *u*, it combines with those letters to make the broad *a* sound. As they are reading and encounter words with *al*, *aw*, or *au*, they should try the /ȧ/ sound.

4. Now direct their attention to the list of hidden objects and again have them notice the different spellings of the broad *a* sound. Emphasize the broad *a* sound as the children find the hidden objects.

Reinforcing /ȧ/

Divide students into cooperative groups of two or three. Give students a copy of "Dinosaur Walk" along with a spinner and tokens. Tell students Jaws the dinosaur is lost and needs help getting home. After spinning, students move the correct number of spaces and read the clue. If the student writes the correct word, he or she stays on that spot. The first person to complete the clues and walks Jaws home is the winner.

Working with Words for /ȧ/

1. Use the following phonograms and words to teach students the sound /ȧ/:

au

caught	fault	taught
caution	naughty	vault
daughter	sausage	

all

ball	gall	wall
call	hall	small
fall	mall	squall
	tall	stall

aw

jaw	raw	flaw
law	saw	slaw
paw	claw	squaw
	draw	straw

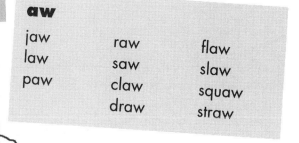

Hidden Pictures

ball 🔴   salt 🧂
chalk ▭   shawl ◿
faucet 🚰   straw ▭
paw 🐾   walkie-talkie 📟

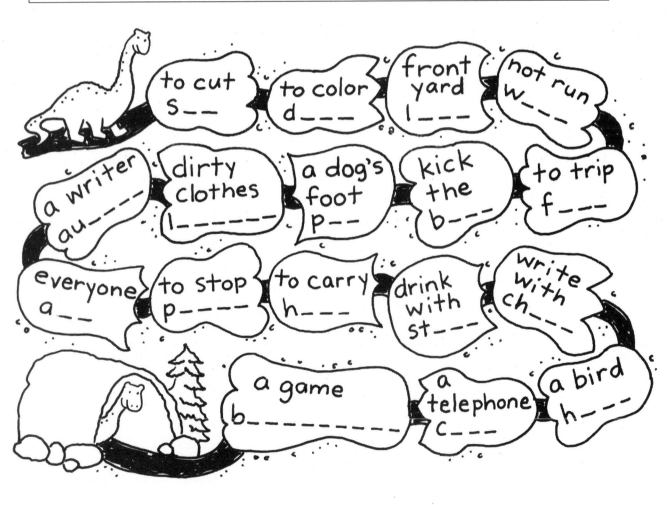
Name_____ Date _____

Dinosaur Walk

Directions: Jaws the dinosaur is lost. She needs your help to get home. Spin the spinner. Use the clue to try and figure out the word. If you figure out the correct word, you move to that spot. The first person to walk Jaws home is the winner.

all	basketball	draw	hawk	pause	straw
author	call	fall	laundry	paw	walk
ball	chalk	haul	lawn	saw	

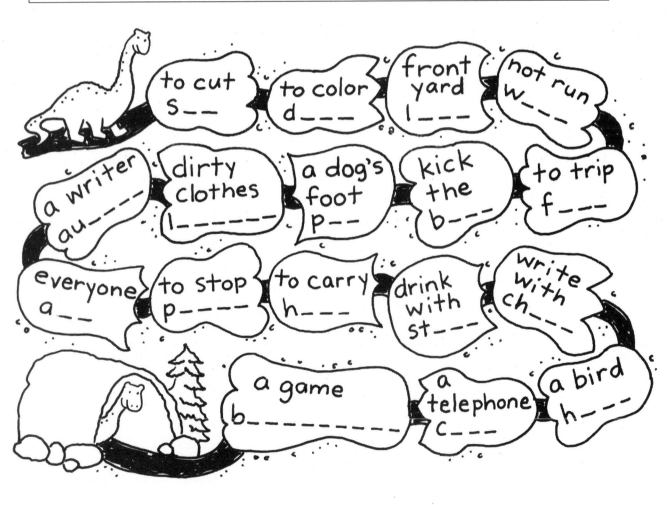

b
as in *ball*

Introducing /b/

1. Blow some bubbles or write the word *bubble* on the board and have the children say it after you. See if they can tell you the beginning sound of *bubbles*. Ask them if they can think of any other words that begin with /b/. If they are not able to do so, tell them to listen to the words you say. Say *bad, bat, baby, boy, bun, bear, best,* and *buy.* Write these words on the board and have the children notice that they all begin with the same letter—*b*. Tell them the letter *b* has the sound /b/.

2. Tell the children you have pictures of lots of things that begin with /b/. Show the children the list of the hidden objects. Have them name each object and trace the *b*s to notice how each word begins. Now direct the children to find the hidden objects in the picture.

Reinforcing /b/

Hand out the reinforcement activity, "Birthday Boy!" Tell the children Bob, the birthday boy, got lots of presents on his birthday and that all begin with /b/. Ask the children to find and color Bob's presents. As the children tell you what they found, emphasize the /b/. They should find a bucket, boat, boots, bat, bulldozer, barn, ball, and book.

Working with Words for /b/

1. Use the following words and common phonograms to help children learn the sound /b/ in the initial position.

bay	bill	bat	bag
back	bank	bell	bunk
bail	by	bug	bin
best	bed	bake	bum

2. When appropriate, teach the children that *b* can be combined with either *l* or *r* to make a consonant blend. Use some words from one of the following lists for the "Working with Words" activity, and have the children notice how they sound at the beginning. See if the children can isolate the /bl/ or /br/ blend. Say the consonant blends slowly so the children can hear the separate sounds of each of the letters and realize what sounds are blended to form the blend. Tell the children that when they see *bl* or *br*, they should not say separate sounds, but rather blend the sounds together. Words you can use for the "Working with Words" activity to reinforce *bl* and *br* are as follows:

br

brace	brow	brick
break	bruise	brag
brass	brittle	broil
bribe	broom	bright
brown	bracelet	brave
bridge	broad	brush
brain	breath	brief
brand	brew	brilliant
brother	bring	brownie

bl

black	bleed	blond
blame	bless	bloom
block	blast	blister
blood	blanket	blow
blue	blade	blend
blunder	blind	blossom
blouse	blaze	blob
bluff	blink	bleach

3. Have the children notice that /b/ is found in the final position in some words. Say the following words for the children and have them repeat the words after you, so they become aware of the /b/ in the final position. Use the "Working with Words" activity so the children can associate /b/ with *b*.

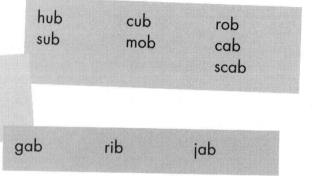

hub   cub   rob
sub   mob   cab
                scab

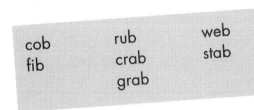

cob   rub   web
fib   crab   stab
        grab

gab   rib   jab

Hidden Pictures

ball ◎   bird 🐦
balloon 🎈   book 📕
bat ⚾   bottle 🍾
bell 🔔   box 📦
belt 👝   bucket 🪣
bib 🦪   bug 🐞

Name_____ Date_____

Birthday Boy!

Directions: Bob got many presents for his birthday. We know what he got because all of the presents begin with /b/, as does his name. Find all the things that begin with /b/. Color them and you will know what Bob got for his birthday.

= /k/, as in *cat*

■ ■ ■ ■ ■ ■ ■ ■ ■ ■ ■ ■ ■ ■ ■ ■ ■ ■ ■ ■

Introducing the /k/ Sound of *c*

1. Introduce the /k/ sound of *c* by giving each child a *cookie*. After the children have enjoyed the cookies, ask them what sound they hear at the beginning of the word *cookie*. Write the word *cookie* on the board and tell the children that one of the sounds *c* makes is /k/, as in *cookie*.

2. Show the children the list of the hidden objects. Have them name the objects and notice the /k/ sound. Then direct the children to find the objects in the hidden picture. Help the children notice that all of the words begin with *c* and have the /k/ sound. Ask them to trace the letter *c* as they say the words. Tell them that when they see a *c*, they can try the /k/ sound. Later you will teach them another sound that *c* makes.

Reinforcing the /k/ Sound of c

1. Ask the children to find the marbles that belong to each child. The marbles that belong to Carl should be colored red, Corky's should be blue, and Curly's should be yellow. The children should draw a smiling face on the child with the most marbles.

2. The children will find that Carl won with *cat, can't, cake, care, camp, came, car, call, card,* and *can.* As the children read the words on the marbles that each child found, they will again have a chance to associate *c* with /k/. The children will also begin to learn that to find out what sound *c* has, you must look at the vowel that follows it; when *c* is followed by *a, o,* or *u,* it usually has the /k/ sound.

Working with Words for the /k/ Sound of *c*

1. Use the following words and common phonograms to help children recognize the sound of /k/.

cat	cap	core
cop	can	cot
cow	cob	
cab	cake	

2. The letter *c* can be combined with either *l* or *r* to form a consonant blend. Read the following words and have the children notice the *cl* or *cr* blend. Help them realize that they are saying /kl/ or /kr/ as they say the words. Use some of these words to teach the children the sound of /k/.

cr

crab	crash	credit
crawl	creek	crown
crooked	crocodile	crumb
crop	crush	crank
crisp	crow	crack
cradle	crayon	creep
cramp	crazy	crib
cream	cross	cry

cl

claim	classroom	clerk
clam	clatter	clever
clarinet	claw	click
climate	closet	clash
clobber	clown	club
clock	clue	clap
close	clutter	clay
clean	climb	class

Hidden Pictures

cake
can
candle
candy cane
cannon
car

card
coin
comb
cone
cube
cupcake

Name_____   Date_____

Playing Marbles

Directions: Carl, Corky, and Curly are playing marbles. All the marbles with words that begin with *ca* belong to Carl. Color them red. The words that begin with *co* are Corky's. Color them blue. The words that begin with *cu* are Curly's. Color them yellow. Draw a happy face on the player who has the most marbles.

C = /s/, as in *circle*

Introducing the /s/ Sound of *c*

1. Ask the children to say some words that begin with the letter *c*. Write the words that they say on the board. If the children cannot think of many words, provide some for them, such as *cut, cement, circle, city, cake, coke,* and *cat.*

2. Tell the children to listen carefully as you read the words. Ask them to notice what sound they hear at the beginning of each word. Children should recognize the /k/, which was taught earlier. They should also realize that some of the words begin with /s/. If not, tell them so and

read the words again as they listen. Lead the children to realize that the letter *c* does not make its own sound, but sounds *either* like /k/ or /s/.

3. Tell the children you know a secret way of finding out whether the *c* sounds like /s/ or /k/. Describe how someone once told you to look at the letter that follows the *c* in order to find out whether to say /k/ or /s/. Now make two separate lists of the words the children gave you earlier. List the words that have the /k/ sound in one column and the words with the /s/ sound in the other column. Have the children notice what letters follow *c* when it has the /k/ sound. Then have the children notice what letters follow *c* when it sounds like /s/. Lead them to realize that when *c* is followed by *a, o,* or *u,* it usually has the /k/ sound. When *c* is followed by *e, i,* or *y,* it usually has the /s/ sound.

Reinforcing the /s/ Sound of *c*

Duplicate the activity sheet with the hidden words. Direct the children to find the six words that begin with the /s/ sound of *c* (*city, cyclone, cement, circus, cycle, cent*) and the six words that begin with the /k/ sound of *c* (*cat, cute, coat, can, cut, cost*). Have them name each list by writing *k* or *s* above it. Summarize the activity by having the children indicate what they should do when they come to a word that has a *c* it. Then have the children find words in their books that follow this principle.

Working with Words for the /s/ Sound of *c*

1. Have children notice that *c* is found in many positions in words. Help them realize that the principle that was taught above is true regardless of the position of the letter *c* in a word. You can use the following words during your "Working with Words" activity to illustrate the /s/ sound of *c* in different positions. Read the words and have the children notice the /s/ sound of *c* and why it has that particular sound.

Again, they will be pointing out that *c* has the /s/ sound when followed by *e, i,* or *y.*

nice	receive	face
niece	except	chance
certain	celery	dance
glance	difference	fence
convince	since	accident
cell	center	

Hidden Pictures

cent
cereal
certificate
cider
cigar

circle
circus
city
cylinder
cymbal

Name_____ Date _____

Hidden Words

Directions: Find six words that begin with c and go across. Find six words that begin with c and go down. Write the words in the correct list below. Complete the sentences to show that you know what to do when you come to a word that has a c in it.

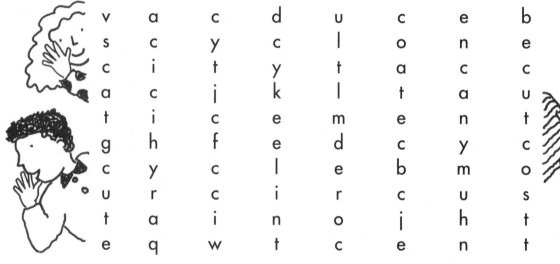

v	a	c	d	u	c	e	b
s	c	y	c	l	o	n	e
c	i	t	y	t	a	c	c
a	c	j	k	l	t	a	u
t	i	c	e	m	e	n	t
g	h	f	e	d	c	y	c
c	y	c	l	e	b	m	o
u	r	c	i	r	c	u	s
t	a	i	n	o	j	h	t
e	q	w	t	c	e	n	t

Words beginning with c going across

1. _____
2. _____
3. _____
4. _____
5. _____
6. _____

Words beginning with c going down

1. _____
2. _____
3. _____
4. _____
5. _____
6. _____

When I come to a word with a c followed by the letter a, o, or u, I should say the ____ sound.

When I come to a word that has a c followed by the letters e, i, or y, I should say the ____ sound.

as in *chain*

 # Introducing /ch/

1. Tell the children that sometimes two consonants combine to make a *new* sound that is not a consonant blend. Review the meaning of a consonant blend by reviewing /br/. As you say /br/, tell the children to listen carefully to the sound of the /b/ and the /r/. Have them notice that they hear a little bit of /b/ and a little bit of /r/ as the sounds are blended.

2. Say that when *c* and *h* come together they also make one sound, but it is not a blend of *c* and *h*. It is a new sound. Ask them to say "choo-choo," so they have an opportunity to say /ch/. Ask them to listen to the sound of ch as you say the following words

and write them on the board: *chair, chain, chalk, change,* and *chin.* Then have them say these words with you.

3. Have the children think of any other words that have the /ch/ sound at the beginning. They may suggest *chap, choose, church, channel, chief, chocolate, chip,* and *cheap.* If not, you can suggest these words so they get to hear the sound again.

4. Now turn to the list of hidden objects. Have the children name the objects they are to find and trace the *ch* as they say the words. Repeat this procedure as they find the objects in the picture.

Reinforcing /ch/

1. Direct the children to find out which train on the reinforcement activity "Choo-Choo-Choo" is carrying more words by finding the words in each line of letters. The children will notice that all of the words begin or end with /ch/. Give examples of words ending in /ch/, such as *much*, *itch*, and *such*.

2. In Chuck's train, they will find *ranch*, *chair*, *rich*, *chat*, *touch*, *change*, *each*, and *champ*. In Chad's they will find *charm*, *much*, *chip*, *porch*, *chew*, *wrench*, and *choose*.

3. Have the children pronounce the words after they have found them, emphasizing the /ch/ at the beginning or end of each word. Use each word in a sentence.

Working with Words for /ch/

1. Common sound patterns you can teach with /ch/ include:

chill	chat	chap
chip	chick	chunk

chain	chop	chest
chug	chin	chow

chew	Chuck	chum
chore		

2. Additional words you can use in teaching /ch/ are:

chair	chocolate	chose

champ	channel	child

chance	choice	chicken
church		

chapel	charge	champ

chalk	choose	cheer
change	choke	chief

lunch	much	pinch
ranch	inch	such

Hidden Pictures

chain
chair
chalk
checkers
cheese
cherries
chicken
chimney
chipmunk

Name_____ Date_____

Choo-Choo-Choo!

Directions: Chuck and Chad have trains. Each train is carrying words that begin or end with /ch/, such as *choo-choo*. Find out whose train is carrying more words by finding the words in each one. Write these words on each train and make a happy face on the engine of the train that is carrying more words. Make a sad face on the train with fewer words. Use the words in sentences.

Chuck   ranchairichatouchangeachamp

1. _____   5. _____
2. _____   6. _____
3. _____   7. _____
4. _____   8. _____

Chad   charmuchiporchewrenchoose

1. _____   5. _____
2. _____   6. _____
3. _____   7. _____
4. _____   8. _____

d

as in *dog*

Introducing /d/

1. Ask the children to listen to /d/ as you read and write the following words: *dart, dash, dog, deer, deep, dent, dig, desk, door, dirt,* and *down.* Have the children repeat each word and then say /d/. Point out the letter *d* in every word on the chalkboard so the children can begin to associate the sound with the symbol.

2. Direct the children's attention to the list of hidden objects. Read each object and again have them notice that each word begins with a *d.* Now have the children find the objects in the hidden picture.

Reinforcing /d/

1. Give each child a copy of "Delightful Dogs." The children can think of names of dogs that begin with /d/, such as *Disney*, *Daisy*, *Daffy*, and *Dover*. Define the word *delightful* by saying it means "being very happy or doing something to please someone." Tell the children the dogs are delightful because they can do all kinds of tricks that begin with /d/. Have the children tell you what the dogs are doing. Write their responses on the board. If a child says "eating"

for "dining," tell her all the tricks begin with /d/ as in "delightful dogs," and then ask for another word for "eating" that begins with /d/.

2. After the children are aware of the tricks and have noticed /d/ at the beginning of every word, direct them to carefully cut out the words and match them with each dog. This activity is self-correcting because the words match the size of the space by each dog.

Working with Words for /d/

1. Words you can use in teaching /d/ in the initial position with common phonograms include:

day dip dunk dot dug dunk

Dan dew dock dim duck deed

dam dill Dick dell ding dine

2. The letter *d* forms sound patterns in many words when it is in the final position, as in the following words. Use the sound patterns (such as /ad/) and add consonants to make words with /d/ in the final position.

ed

bed	red	sled
fed	shed	sped
led		

ad

add	glad	mad
bad	had	pad
dad	lad	sad

id

bid	kid	skid
did	lid	slid
hid	rid	

Text copyright © Harry W. Forgan and James W. Forgan. Illustrations copyright © Pearson Learning.

3. *D* can be combined with *r* to make the *dr* consonant blend. Use the following words during your "Working with Words" activity so the children can learn this consonant blend.

draft
drill
drama
drop
dream
drug

dry
drain
drip
drawer
drowned
dribble

draw
drove
dress
dragon
drink
drapery

Hidden Pictures

dart
desk
diamond
dime
dog
door
duck

Name_____ Date_____

Delightful Dogs

Directions: These dogs are delightful! They are happy because they are doing their best tricks. Look at the dogs and then match the word with each dog's trick. Cut out the words and paste them by the trick each dog is doing. Make sure your word fits into the box by each dog.

| dating | digging | dining | diving |
| dusting | dialing | dancing | |

ĕ
as in egg

Introducing /ĕ/

1. Tell the children you have a secret message for them. They can figure out what the message is by adding the letter *e*. Write these letters on the board as shown. (When the messages are completed, they should read: *get wet, get set, send help, bet yes,* and *step left.*)

```
    w         s              h
g       t   g       t   s       nd
    t           t           l
                            p
        y                   l
    b   t               st  p
    s                       f
                            t
```

2. Say that today you are going to help them learn the short *e* sound. Tell them short *e* is /ĕ/, as in *get* and *set.* Inform them that short *e* is a different sound than long *e*. Tell them you are now going to say some other words. If the word you say has a short *e*, they should clap. Say the following words: *ten, let, please, slept, dear, eat, met, went, end,* and *bed.*

3. Now direct the children's attention to the list of hidden objects. Again, have them notice the /ĕ/ sound and emphasize it as they find the objects in the picture.

Text copyright © Harry W. Forgan and James W. Forgan. Illustrations copyright © Pearson Learning.

Reinforcing /ĕ/

We've provided a crossword puzzle to reinforce the short e sound. Tell the children to follow the dots in each box to figure out what the object is. After they know what it is, they should write its name in the appropriate space. If this is the children's first experience with a crossword puzzle, you may want to do it with them. Have them say the words that are in the puzzle (*puzzle, bell, belt, tent,* and *egg*) and again emphasize the /ĕ/ sound. Ask the children whether they can think of words that rhyme with these objects and thus have the /ĕ/ sound.

Working with Words for /ĕ/

1. Use these words to teach frequently appearing phonograms with short e.

est

best	test	crest
nest	vest	chest
rest	pest	quest

ell

bell	sell	smell
cell	tell	shell
fell	well	spell
	yell	swell

ed

bed	led	bled
fed	Fred	fled
red	Ted	wed
		sled

2. Additional phonograms for short *e* include:

en

Ben	men	Glen
den	pen	then
hen	ten	when
Ken		

end

bend	mend	blend
end	send	spend
lend	tend	

ent

bent	Kent	sent
cent	lent	vent
dent	rent	went
		scent

ess

guess	bless	dress
less	chess	press
mess		stress

et

bet	let	pet
get	met	set
jet	net	wet
		yet

3. In about nine of ten words, the *e* is short because it is in a closed syllable (CVC). A closed syllable is a syllable that ends in a consonant. Tell the children that when they come to a word or syllable that has one *e* and they notice that the word or syllable ends in a consonant, they should try /ĕ/. Sample words that you can use in your "Working with Words" activity to teach this generalization are as follows:

One Syllable		Two Syllables (first syllable has /ĕ/)
dress	them	seven
less	then	pebble
best	den	checkers
chest	men	freckles
rest	egg	medal
test	tent	beggar
get	went	shelter
let	pep	tennis
net	smell	pencil
pet	swell	center
met	peck	
set	deck	
wet	neck	
yet	left	
help	leg	

Hidden Pictures

bed
bench
bread
egg

nest
sled
tent

Name_____ Date_____

Dot and Cross

Directions: Follow the dots. Write the names of the pictures you drew in the puzzle. Use each word in a sentence.

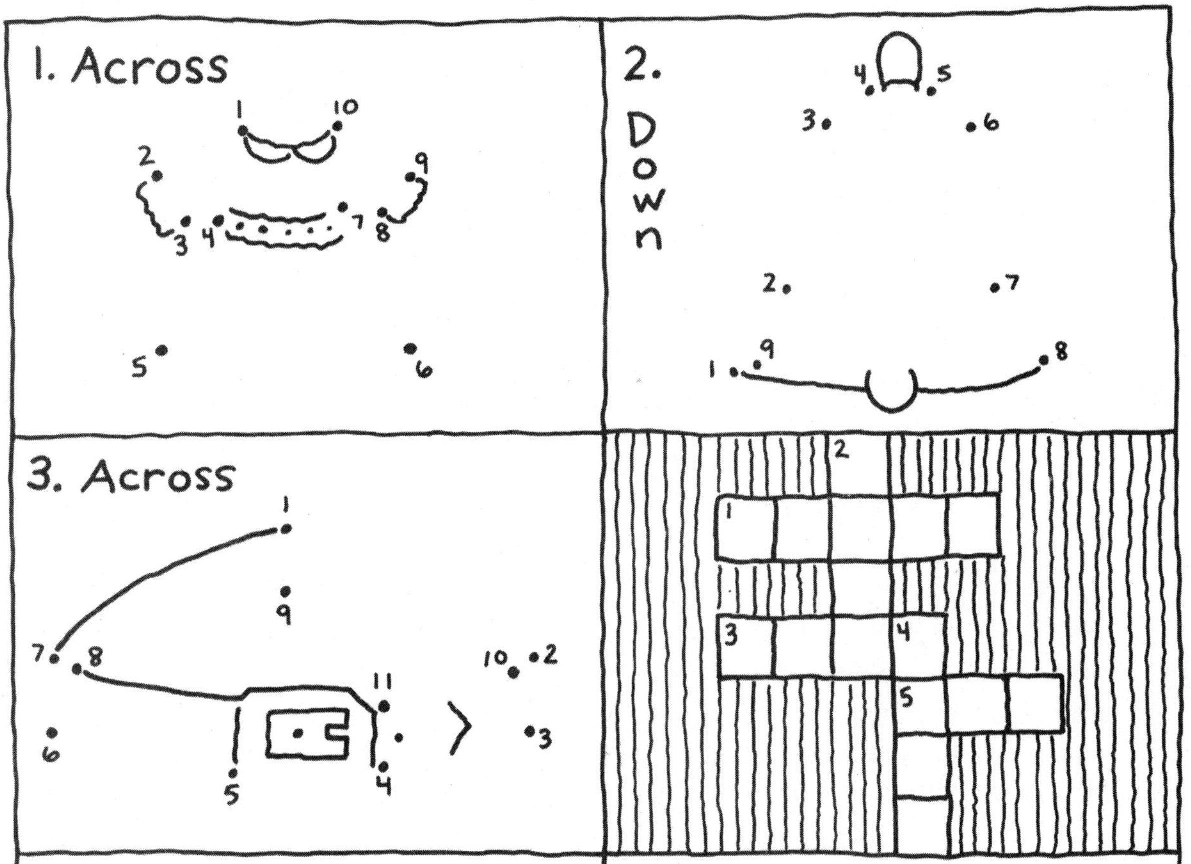

1. Across

2. Down

3. Across

4. Down

5. Across

as in *tree*

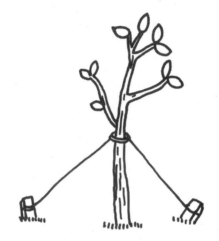

■ ■

 # Introducing /ē/

1. Tell the children you are going to read a story about three pigs. The problem is that every once in a while you come to a word that you cannot read. Write the word on the board or draw a picture, and ask whether the children can tell you what it is. Tell them that all of these words will have an /ē/ sound in them. Read the following story, leaving out the words in parentheses.

The (three) little pigs were happy. The wolf was gone and they were (free). That night they had food to (eat) and (tea) to drink. After their (meal), they all decided to (read).

One pig noticed a bright star shining in the (east). He saw the star because their roof had a (leak). Soon one pig saw the wolf (peeking) through the hole. The other pig said, "Here (we) go!" Just then they heard the wolf fall, and the pigs said, "That should (teach) him!"

2. After you have listed all of the words from this chalk talk, have the children listen as you read the words to notice the /ē/ sound. Have them say the words after you so they have a chance to say /ē/. You can point out that /ē/ sounds like its letter name.

3. Now direct the children's attention to the list of the hidden objects. Have them say the words and notice the /ē/.

Reinforcing /ē/

Divide students into cooperative groups of two or three. Give students a copy of "Ethan Eats" along with a spinner and tokens. Tell students that Ethan can only eat things that have the /ē/ sound. Students take turns spinning and moving their tokens. If the student can determine if the word has the long *e* sound and can be eaten, they stay on that spot. If they cannot, they return to their previous position. The first person to the end is the winner.

Working with Words for /ē/

1. This is a good time to review the principle that when *ee* and *ea* occur together, usually the first letter is long and the second letter is silent. Use these patterns in your "Working with Words" activity:

e

be	he	we
	me	she

eak

bleak	teak	speak
leak	weak	squeak
peak	freak	streak
	sneak	tweak

each

beach	reach	bleach
peach	teach	preach

eal

deal	real	squeal
heal	seal	steal
meal	veal	

ean

bean	Jean	mean
Dean	lean	clean

eat

beat   meat   cheat
heat   neat   cleat
           seat   pleat

eed

deed   seed   breed
feed   weed   freed
need   bleed   greed

eek

peek   seek   cheek
        week   creek

eel

feel   peel   steel
kneel   reel   wheel

eep

beep   jeep   seep
deep   keep   weep
        peep

eet

beet   meet   street
feet   greet   sweet
        sheet

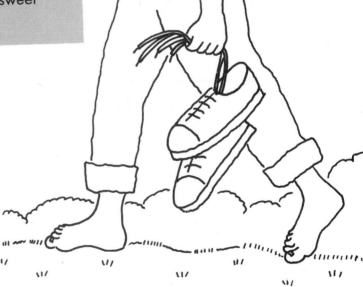

Hidden Pictures

bee
cheese
leaf
seal
three
tree
wheel
tepee

Name_____ Date_____

Ethan Eats

Directions: Ethan can only eat things that have the long *e* sound. He needs your help to decide what to eat! Spin and move your token. Say the word aloud. Does the word have the long *e* sound? Is the word something Ethan can eat? If you answer correctly, you stay on that spot; if not, you go back. The first person to the end is the winner.

ẽr

as in *bird*

Introducing /ẽr/

1. Ask the children if they have ever listened to a dog before the dog began to bark. Ask them what sound the dog made. They should say /ẽr/. If not, illustrate this sound to them by pretending that you are a dog who has heard something, and begin to say /ẽr/—/ẽr/—/ẽr/.

2. Tell the children that this is one of the sounds in our language. If dogs knew a few more sounds they could say words, because many words have /ẽr/. Tell them to listen to /ẽr/

as you say these words: *bird, skirt, church, hurt, word, fur, were, worm,* and *turn*. Write these words on the board to show the different spellings of /ẽr/: *her, sir, fur,* and *word*. Tell the children that *er, ir, ur,* and *(w)or* can sound like /ẽr/.

3. Now direct their attention to the list of the hidden objects. They should notice that all of the words have /ẽr/ spelled with *er, ir,* or *ur*. As the children find the objects, have them again emphasize the /ẽr/.

Reinforcing /ẽr/

Give each student a copy of "Earthly Invaders." Read each word aloud with the class. Tell students they will help the invaders capture all the words with the /ẽr/ sound by circling or highlighting those words.

Working with Words for /ẽr/

The children may need more review on the ways /ẽr/ can be spelled in different words. You can use the words in the following columns to indicate each phonogram or word family.

ir

stir	dirt	sir
birth	firm	girl
bird	skirt	dirt
third	squirt	shirt
swirl	fir	

er

were	serve	fern
her	jerk	germ
verse	mother	learn
father	sister	verb
nerve	clerk	

ur

fur	church	blur
purr	curve	curb
nurse	hurt	curl
turn	turkey	purge
burn	burn	urge

wor

worse	worth	worry
worm	work	worship
word	world	wordy

Hidden Pictures

bird circle earthworm purse shirt skirt turnip turtle

Name_____ Date_____

Earthly Invaders

Directions: Help the earthly invaders capture all of the words with the /ẽr/ sound. Read each word aloud. If the word has the /ẽr/ sound, color or highlight it to help the invaders find the word.

water	nurse	pool
bird	school	camera
baby	purse	car
girl	shirt	river
cat	house	water
church	mom	chair
turkey	skirt	turtle
fish	thirteen	earthworm

êr

as in ear

Introducing /êr/

1. Tell the children that one sound in the English language sounds like something on their heads. Tell them to listen as you read a story that has many words that sound like *ear*. Ask them to listen and see whether they can *hear* the sound (write the word *hear* on the board). Say the story is about two *deer* talking (write the word *deer* on the board). The father deer is talking to the baby deer.

Say, "My *dear*, I get a *tear* when I hear about your *fear*. It is *clear* that a *spear* can put a hole in the *rear* of

a deer! But don't be *weary*, a *deer* has good *ears!* You will *hear* the hunter when he lets out a *cheer!* He will say, 'A *deer* is *here!*' You will say, 'I'm getting out of *here!*'"

2. Ask the children what words they heard that have the /êr/ sound. See if they can think of any other words. If not, refer them to the list of hidden objects. As they say the names of the objects, they will hear /êr/. After they have found the objects, review the sound and ways in which it can be spelled.

Reinforcing /êr/

Tell the children you have a picture of a clown who likes to wear lots of hats. Say they can give him lots of hats if they can make words that have /êr/. Hand out the reinforcement activity, "Hats Off!" Ask the children to take the letters from one *ear* and combine them with *ear* to make words. They should write each word on a hat and trace the hat. After the children have written the words on the hats, have them read the words and use them in sentences. Tell them that when they come to a word that has *ear*, they should try /êr/.

Working with Words for /êr/

Generally the *ear* combination does make the /êr/ sound; however, this sound can also be produced by the *eer* combination. Words you can use during your "Working with Words" activities to teach the *eer* and *ear* combinations are:

eer

deer	queer	jeer
peer	sneer	cheer
	steer	

ear

dear	near	clear
fear	rear	smear
gear	tear	spear
hear	year	shear

Hidden Pictures

beard
ear
earring
mirror
spear
tear

Name_____ Date_____

Hats Off!

Directions: This clown likes to wear hats. His hats are off right now. You can give him new hats by finding a sound in the left ear and adding it in front of *ear* in the right ear. Write the new word on one of the hats and then trace around the dots to complete the hat. See how many hats you can give this clown. Use each word in a sentence.

as in *foot*

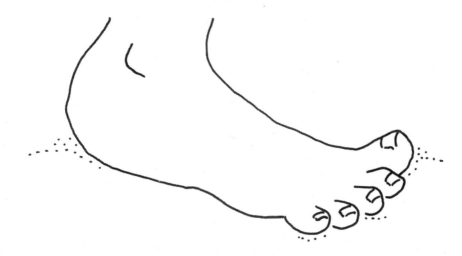

Introducing /f/

1. Ask the children what sound a cat makes when it is angry. Tell them this sound is like /f/, which is heard in many words. Tell them to listen to you make the sound of the angry cat as you read the following words: *fight, fox, favorite, five, four, fan, fair, fail,* and *fire.*

2. Say the words again and have the children say each one after you. Write the letter *f* on the board along with the words that you have said. Tell the children that when they see the letter *f*, they should say /f/.

3. You can have them feel this sound by noticing how their upper teeth rest on their lower lip when they begin to say the sound. Also have them notice how their mouth opens as they say the sound.

4. Direct the children's attention to the list of the hidden objects. Have them say the name of each object and trace the *f* in the written word. Now have the children find the hidden objects in the picture and say the words as they find them. Write *f* on the board again and tell the children that when they see an *f*, they should say /f/ as in *feathers.*

Reinforcing /f/

Duplicate the reinforcement activity, "Football Field Goals," and ask the children to find the hidden words that go across and begin with /f/. When they find a word they can read, they should write it on one of the footballs. Tell them to see whether they can kick a field goal by finding at least 8 words that begin with /f/. Some of the students may be able to find 16 words and thus score two field goals. Have them read the words to one another so they can listen to the /f/.

Working with Words for /f/

1. Words containing common phonograms you can use to teach /f/ in the initial position are:

fat	fed	fell	fake	Fay
feed	fight	fan	fine	
few	fill	fin	fail	

2. Help the children realize /f/ is also found in the final position in some words. You can use the following list of words and ask the children to listen to the final sounds as you read them. Use these words in your "Working with Words" activity so the children can see the letter *f* in the final position:

calf	chef	cuff	off	if
chief	grief	thief	puff	wife
half	deaf	beef	stuff	

f

3. The children will soon be aware of the fact that *f* can be combined with *l* or *r* to form a consonant blend. Help the children realize that a little bit of each one of the sounds makes the blend. You may want to emphasize the *f* and *l* sounds as you say words such as *flag*, *fly*, and *float*. The children will be able to hear a little bit of the /f/ and /r/ in such words as *free*, *front*, and *fruit*. Other words you can use to help the children hear the *fl* and *fr* consonant blends are:

fl

flat	flame	flannel	flies
flight	flavor	fleas	flashlight
flower	flip	fluff	flock
	flour		flush

fr

frame	fresh	freeze
French fries	frill	friend
fright	frog	from
frost		

Hidden Pictures

face 😊
fan
feather
fence
finger
firecracker

fish
foot
football
footstool
fork
funnel

Name_____ Date_____

Football Field Goals

Directions: Can you kick a field goal over the bar? Find the hidden words that begin with *f* and go across. Write each word on a football. You will need to find at least eight words to make one good kick. You may be able to make two good kicks if you can find eight more words. Have fun finding the words.

g

as in *ghost*

Introducing /g/

1. Write the letter *g* on the board. Under it write the following words: *go, gas, give, got, gum.* Tell the children to listen to each of the words as you read them and notice the sound at the beginning. After you have read the words to the children, ask them what sound the letter *g* makes. See if they can think of any other words that begin with /g/. You may want to suggest some, such as *goose, garbage, gang, game, get,* *guard,* and *gold.* Have the children write the letter *g* and say its sound.

2. Now direct the children's attention to the hidden objects list. Have them notice that each word begins with /g/. Tell the children to say the words and trace the *g*. Now direct the children to find the hidden objects, and say what they have found and what sound the names of the objects have at the beginning.

Reinforcing /g/

Duplicate the "Go, Go, Go!" game. Provide the children with a die and tokens. Tell them to put their tokens on Start. One child begins by throwing a die. She moves her token to the new space and reads the instructions there.

The first one who gets to the end is the winner. Notice that the children will be reading /g/ many times as they play this game. Have them point out all the words that have the /g/ sound and use them in sentences.

Working with Words for /g/

1. The sound of /g/ is often heard in the final position of words. Use the phonograms of *ag*, *eg*, *ig*, *og*, and *ug* in your "Working with Words" activity. As students make the new words, have them point out the /g/ at the end of the words. Words you can use are:

eg
beg
egg   leg
keg   peg

ag
bag   nag   snag
flag   rag   tag
gag   shag

og
dog
fog   hog
frog   log

ig
big   fig   swig
dig   pig   twig
        rig   wig

ug
bug   dug   plug
chug   hug   tug
drug   mug

2. Words with /g/ in the initial position include:

gay	gail
gill	gain
gag	gab
got	gum
gap	

gl

glad	glare	glitter	globe
glance	glass	glory	glove
glow	glue		

gr

grab	grade	grapes	gravel
grit	ground	grace	grand
gray	grease	groom	grow
green	greet	grill	grin
gravy	grass	great	growl

3. *G* can be combined with either *l* or *r* to form a consonant blend. You might want to say the blend slowly so the children can hear a little bit of each of the sounds that are blended together to make one sound. Help the children realize that they should say only one sound when they see *gl* or *gr*. Use the following words to help the children hear the *gl* and *gr* consonant blends.

Hidden Pictures

gate 🔲
ghost 👻
girl 👧
goat 🐐
goggles 👓
goose 🦢
guitar 🎸
gum ▭

Name_____ Date_____

Go, Go, Go!

Directions: You will need a die and tokens for each player. Decide who goes first. Throw the die to see how many spaces you can move. You must do what the space tells you to do. The first to reach "Good! You are the winner!" on the exact count wins.

Start

Good! Go ahead 2.

Good! You gave the girl gold. Go ahead 1.

Get gas here and go-go-go.

Get Out! Go back 1.

Give the others a chance. Go back 1.

Get going! Go ahead 1.

FREE

FREE

FREE

Good! You are the Winner!

You cannot win this game so soon. Go back 4.

Go back 1. You are going too fast. The guard got you!

You got by. Go ahead 1 more.

FREE

Chewing gum? Go back 3.

Go ahead 2. The gang goes for you!

h
as in *hat*

Introducing /h/

1. Read the following sentences to the children and ask them to listen for the sound they hear again and again.

The hairy hippo has hot honey.

The huge horse hit a happy hippo.

The haunted house on the hill is the home of a happy hog.

He hit the horn with his hand.

If the children are unable to point out the /h/ sound, write *h* on the board and say its sound. Read some of the sentences again.

2. Write the words that begin with *h.* Use such nouns as *hippopotamus, hammer, honey,* and *house* in one column. In another column write such verbs as *have, hurt, has, help, hit,* and *hold.* Make a third column of words that can be used as adjectives, such as *husky, happy, hard,* and *haunted.* See whether the children can make up some of their own sentences with as many words as possible beginning with /h/. When the sentences are read, have the other children listen to the /h/ sound.

3. Distribute the list of the hidden objects. Have the children say the name of each object and trace the letter *h* at the beginning of each word. Direct the children to find the objects in the picture, and emphasize the /h/ as they tell you what they have found.

Reinforcing /h/

Duplicate the reinforcement activity, "The Haunted House." See whether the children can find their way home from the haunted house by reading each of the words that begins with /h/. Players can spin a spinner or throw a die to see how many spaces they may move. In order to move, they must read the word or at least say the /h/. The first one to get home is the winner. Read the words again with the children so they can hear the /h/ sound. Have children use each word in a sentence.

Working with Words for /h/

Frequently appearing words you can use to teach /h/ are:

he	had	help	happy	hill
his	here	hold	hard	ham
had	house	hot	hope	hug
have	home	hurt	hear	how
her	high	hat	head	him
hum	hay	hop	heed	how
hip				

Hidden Pictures

hair
ham
hand
hanger
harp

hay
head
heart
hen

Name_____ Date_____

The Haunted House

Directions: Can you find your way home from the haunted house? Spin your spinner to see how many spaces you can move. When you land on a space, you must say the word. The first one "home" on the exact count is the winner.

as in *fish*

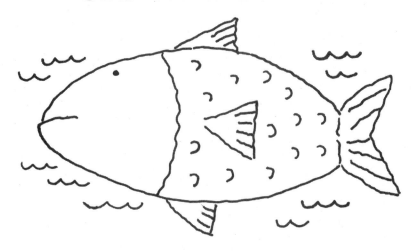

■ ■

 # Introducing / ĭ /

1. You can introduce this sound by telling the children that today they are going to play tag. One child is "It." She tries to tag other children by reading their word cards.

2. To play this game, you first give each child a card with a word that has the letter *i* in it. Some of the word cards should have the short *i* sound and some should have the long *i* sound. For example, you might want to pass out cards with these words: *if, in, did, is, his, win* (short *i* words) and *I, like, nine, bite,* and

nice (long *i* words). Tell the children the person who is It can tag only the children whose cards have the sound of *i* as in *it.* To tag a person, you must read his or her word. The children who have a long *i* word cannot be tagged.

3. After the children have exchanged cards and had turns being It, have them again review the words with / ĭ /. Now direct their attention to the list of hidden objects and again have them notice the / ĭ / sound.

Reinforcing / ĭ /

Give each student a copy of "Happy Hippie the Clown." Tell students they will use the words in the word box to complete the story. Read each word aloud with the students. When the students are finished, tell them to read their story to a partner.

 # Working with Words for / ĭ /

You can use the common sound patterns in your "Working with Words" activity. Possible words follow:

ib

bib	crib	fib
		rib

ick

kick	lick	chick
sick	pick	flick
stick	tick	slick
trick	brick	thick

id

hid	did	rid
lid	slid	skid
	kid	

it

it	fit	sit
	kit	split

ift

gift	sift	drift
lift	swift	shift

ig

big	pig	jig
dig	twig	rig
	fig	swig

in

fin	spin	chin
pin	twin	grin
win	bin	skin
tin	sin	thin

im

him	slim	Jim
swim	trim	Kim
dim	dim	rim
	brim	Tim

ill

bill	dill	till
hill	fill	will
pill	gill	chill
spill	Jill	drill
thrill	kill	still
	mill	thrill

ing

ding	sting	ring
ping	string	spring
wing	swing	sing
cling	thing	king
sling	wring	bring

ink

drink	think	mink
pink	sink	rink
blink	link	wink
		stink

ip

chip	rip	skip
dip	sip	slip
tip	zip	strip
ship	clip	trip
drip	flip	whip
hip	grip	
lip		

it

bit	hit	skit
fit	lit	slit
kit	pit	spit
	sit	split
	quit	

itch

ditch	itch	stitch
hitch	pitch	

int

hint	tint	sprint
lint	print	squint
mint	splint	

Hidden Pictures

bricks

clip

fish

gift

igloo

inch

pin

ring

Name_____ Date_____

Happy Hippie the Clown

Directions: Use the words in the box to complete the sentences. You may use each word more than one time.

is	inside	did	little	city	big
in	isn't	his	will	begins	invent

This story b _ _ _ _ _ in the c _ _ _. Happy Hippie was

looking for a l _ _ _ _ _ ball to use in his clown show. He

saw lots of b _ _ balls, but no l _ _ _ _ _ balls. Happy

Hippie looked ins _ _ _ every store but d _ _ not see a

l _ _ _ _ _ ball. What w _ _ _ he do? Happy Hippie

i _ _ ' _ happy. He decided to inv _ _ _ a

l _ _ _ _ _ ball to use i _ h _ _ show! Now Happy

Hippie the clown i _ happy!

ī

as in *kite*

■ ■

Introducing / ī /

Ask the children whether they can guess the word people say most often. If the children are not aware that the most frequently spoken word is *I*, tell them so. Tell them also that this is the long sound of *i* and that it is found in many words. Ask them to tell you some words that have / ī /. If they cannot, show them the list of the hidden objects. As you say the names of the objects, emphasize the long *i* sound. After the children have found the objects in the picture with the Thanksgiving scene, have them isolate the long *i* sound in the words and then suggest other words that also include / ī /.

Reinforcing / ī /

Give each student a copy of the "Missing Word" activity. Read aloud the words in the word box, emphasizing that they all have the /ī/ sound. Instruct students to read each clue to determine the missing word.

Working with Words for / ī /

1. Common sound patterns with long *i* include:

ile

file	pile	smile
mile	tile	while

ice

dice	nice	price
lice	rice	slice
mice	vice	splice
		twice

ime

dime	mime	crime
lime	time	prime
	chime	slime

ind

bind	hind	mind
blind	kind	wind
	grind	

ide

hide	tide	glide
ride	wide	pride
side	bride	slide
		stride

ipe

| pipe | wipe | stripe |
| ripe | gripe | swipe |

ite

| bite | kite | site |
| | quite | white |

ive

| dive | hive | live |
| five | jive | drive |

ied

| died | cried | spied |
| lied | fried | tried |

ight

fight	night	bright
knight	right	flight
light	sight	fright
might	tight	

ike

| bike | Mike | spike |
| like | pike | strike |

2. Tell the children that sometimes y represents /ī/. This is true when y is the only vowel at the end of a one-syllable word, as in the following:

cry	try	why	my
dry	shy	sky	by
fly	ply	sly	spy

Hidden Pictures

dice
iron
kite
light
pie
pipe
pliers
tires

Name_____ Date_____

Missing Word

Directions: Use the clues to figure out the words with the long *i* sound.

tiny	ice	silent	pilot	triangle
rifle	lion	mice	spider	dinosaur

Clue   ## Word

1. This is cold.   i __ __

2. This has three sides.   tr __ __ __ __ __ __

3. to be quiet   s __ __ __ __ __

4. a type of gun   r __ __ __ __

5. This person flies a plane.   p __ __ __ __

6. very small   t __ __ __

7. Barney is a ____.   d __ __ __ __ __ __ __

8. king of the jungle   l __ __ __

9. This has eight legs.   sp __ __ __ __

10. three blind ____.   m __ __ __

j
as in *jeep*

Introducing /j/

1. Repeat the poem "Jack and Jill." Tell the children you know some words that begin the way the words *Jack* and *Jill* do. Say "*jail, jacket, judge, join, joke, jump, jewelry, joy,* and *junk.*" Ask the children to tell you what sound they heard at the beginning of each of the words. Write the letter *j* and the above words on the board and again have the children say /j/ when they see the letter *j*. Ask them to think of any other words that being with /j/.

2. Direct their attention to the list of the hidden objects. Have them say the name of each object and again trace the letter *j*. Ask the children to find the hidden objects in the picture and have them say /j/ as they tell you about their discoveries.

Reinforcing /j/

Tell the children they can play jacks, and give them the "Jacks" activity page. Ask them to see how many jacks they can get by finding the word on each jack. If they are able to make a word beginning with /j/, they have won that jack. Have them read *jam*, *joke*, *jet*, *jelly*, *join*, *juggle*, *jar*, *juice* and *jacket*, and again notice the /j/.

Working with Words for /j/

1. Use these words to teach children the sound of /j/:

Jill	jam	Jack	junk	jail
job	jock	Jim	jet	jar
Jay	jug	Jake	jot	jab

2. The children must learn that the letter *g* sometimes represents /j/. Use words such as *gem*, *gerbil*, *giant*, *gyp*, *gingerbread*, *germ*, *general*, and *gentle* to teach this sound. Tell children that to find out whether the *g* stands for /g/ or /j/, they must look at the second letter in the word. Usually if the word has an *e*, *i*, or *y* after the *g*, the /j/ is heard. There are exceptions to this generalization, such as the words *give*, *get*, and *gear*, so make sure you emphasize the word *usually*. This principle is particularly true when *g* is followed by *e* at the end of a word, as in *age*, *gage*, *page*, *wage*, *huge*, *large*, and *barge*.

Hidden Pictures

jacks ✳
jail ▥
jar 🫙
jaws 〰

jeans 👖
jeep 🚙
jet ✈
jug 🪔

Name_____ Date_____

Jacks

Directions: See how many jacks you can get by unscrambling the words. Rearrange the letters so that each word begins with a *j*. Write your word under the jack and then the jack is yours. Use your new words in sentences.

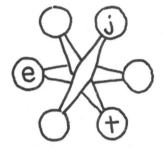

1._____   2._____   3._____

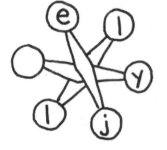

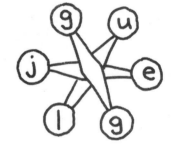

4._____   5._____   6._____

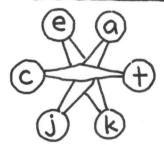

7._____   8._____   9._____

126

k

as in *key*

Introducing /k/

1. If you have already taught the /k/ sound of *c*, the children are familiar with this sound. If not, you might introduce it by asking the children to cough. Usually children will make the /k/ sound when they cough. If not, say /k/.

2. Ask the children whether they can think of any words that begin with /k/. The children may give you words that begin with *ca, co, cu,* or the letter *k*. If not, provide sample words such as the following:

cake	cat	can't	catch
cup	cut	come	cold
kid	key	kite	kit

keep	kick	kind	kiss
cave	cord	kill	king

Direct the children to notice /k/ at the beginning of each of the words. Help them see that both *c* and *k* can represent /k/.

3. Tell the children today they are going to find pictures of words that have the letter *k* at the beginning to stand for /k/. Show them the list of hidden objects and have them trace the letter *k* at the beginning of each word. Have the children find the hidden objects in the picture, and have them emphasize the /k/ as they tell you what they have found.

Reinforcing /k/

Give each student a copy of the "Missing Word" activity. Read aloud the words in the word box, emphasizing that they all have the /k/ sound. Instruct students to read each clue to determine the missing word.

Working with Words for /k/

1. As pointed out in the reinforcement activity, /k/ is heard at the end of many words. Use the sound patterns such as *ack, eck, ick, ock, uck, ike, ake,* and *oke* in your "Working with Words" activity. Have the children add beginning consonants to make words such as those that follow. As the children say the words, help them hear the /k/ at the end. Review the fact that *ck* makes the /k/ sound.

eck
neck   speck   fleck
wreck

ack
back   pack   sack
jack

ock
sock   smock   rock
lock

ick
sick   tick   nick
brick

ake
bake   cake   make
lake

uck
luck   duck   struck
suck

ike
bike   hike   like
strike

oke
broke   woke   coke
poke

2. Words with the most common phonograms that you can use in teaching /k/ in the initial position are:

kick   king   Kim   kin   kite

3. The /k/ sound is blended with *s* to form /sk/ as in *skate, school,* and *scat*. The /sk/ blend can also be found in the final position, as in *ask*. See the lesson plan for the sound of *s* for more words for these blends.

Hidden Pictures

kangaroo
kayak
ketchup
kettle
key
keyhole
kite
kitten

Name_____ Date_____

Missing Word

Directions: Use the clues to figure out the words with the /k/ sound.

king	cat	cut	kind	duck	sick
bike	rock	cake	cup	cave	key
	kite	cold	kangaroo		

Clue   ## Word

1. eat birthday ____   _ _ _ _
2. "meow" says the ____   _ _ _
3. ride a ____   _ _ _ _
4. "quack" says the ____   _ _ _ _
5. drink from a ____   _ _ _
6. this opens a lock ____   _ _ _
7. use scissors to ____   _ _ _
8. lives in a castle ____   _ _ _ _
9. to be nice ____   _ _ _ _
10. fly a ___   _ _ _ _
11. you find this on the ground ____   _ _ _ _
12. not feeling well ____   _ _ _ _
13. ice cream feels ____   _ _ _ _
14. bears sleep in a ____   _ _ _ _
15. this animals hops ____   _ _ _ _ _ _ _ _

1

as in *ladder*

Introducing /l/

1. Tell the children that you are going to sing to them. Tell them that as you sing, you are going to be saying a sound. They should see whether they can find out what sound you are saying. Sing, "*la, la, la, la, la, la, la.*"

2. If the children are not able to isolate the /l/, tell them what sound you were singing by singing it very loudly. Tell the children you are going to say some words that begin with /l/. Ask them to watch your mouth because you will look like a singer even though you do not sound like one. Say these words: *life, live, love,* *late, laugh, lay, lie, like, lick, lunch, luck,* and *look.*

3. Write the words on the board and have the children say them as you point to each one. Help them notice that they open their mouths as they say /l/.

4. You can demonstrate this again as you have the children look at the list of hidden objects. Have them trace the letter *l* as they say the /l/ sound. Tell the children that you will make a list of the objects as they find them. Read the list again together so the children say /l/ again.

Reinforcing /l/

Write the words *ladders* and *loops* on the board. Tell the children you have a game called "Ladders and Loops." You will need to show them how to play it the first time. You need a die and a token for each player or team. Tell the children to take turns throwing the die to see how many spaces to move. They move their tokens and read the words along the way. If the player lands on a "Lucky Ladder," he gets to move forward along the ladder. If he lands on a "Lousy Loop," he must move back in the direction of the loop. The first player to the finish line on the exact count is the winner.

Working with Words for /l/

1. Use the following phonograms to teach the /l/ sound in the initial position.

lay	lip	lick	lot	lap	link
low	led	lock	lake	line	lab
light	luck	Lill	lamb	lack	lob

2. The children will soon recognize that *l* is found in many sound patterns. Use the following phonograms to teach the /l/ sound in the final position.

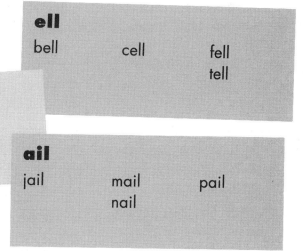

ell
bell   cell   fell
                              tell

ail
jail   mail   pail
            nail

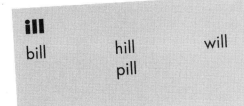

ill
bill   hill   will
            pill

3. The letter *l* is also combined with many consonants to form consonant blends: *bl, cl, fl, gl, pl, sl,* and *spl.* Sample words have been provided for all of the above consonant blends in the lesson plans for the first letter of the blends. *L* is also blended with *d* or *t* in the final position of words or syllables. Use the following words to help children learn the *ld* and *lt* blends:

lt

built	belt	smelt
stilts	felt	colt
quilt	melt	bolt
		adult

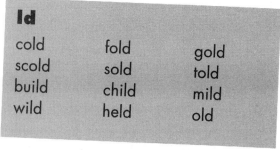

ld

cold	fold	gold
scold	sold	told
build	child	mild
wild	held	old

Hidden Pictures

ladder
ladybug
lamp
lantern
leash
log
leg
lemon
letter
lips
lock

Name_____ Date _____

Ladders and Loops

Directions: You will need a die and tokens for each player or team. Decide who is going to go first. Move as many spaces as the die says. Read each word as you move along. If you land on a lucky ladder you get to move down. If you land on a lousy loop you must move back in the direction of the arrows. The first one to *Laugh* on the exact count is the winner.

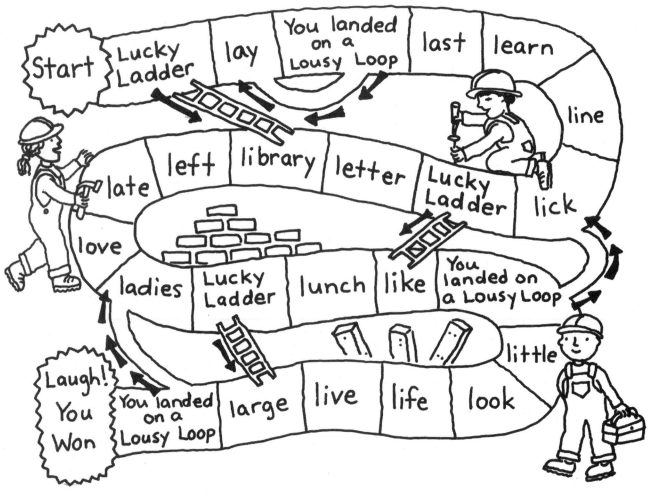

as in *man*

Introducing /m/

1. Ask the children to name some of their favorite people. *Mother, mom, mama, mum,* or *me* will probably come early in the list. Ask the children whether they can think of any other words that begin with /m/. If they cannot, say such words as *mad, may, mailman, map, make, mix, mug, much,* and *mouth.* Tell the children to listen to the sound they hear at the beginning of each of the words as you read them again.

2. Write the words *my, may, more,* and *mad* on the board and point

out the letter *m* as the children say the words after you. Write the letter *m* on the board and have the children say the /m/. You might have the children feel how their lips are together and then open up as they say the /m/.

3. Tell the children that the objects in the hidden picture all begin with /m/. Go over the list of objects and have the children say each one and trace the *m*s. Ask the children to find the hidden objects in the picture. As they find the objects, emphasize the /m/ sound.

Reinforcing /m/

Duplicate the "Matching Monkeys" page and give a copy to each child. Ask the children to look at the pictures of the monkeys to find out what they are doing. Tell them each monkey is doing something that begins with /m/, as in *monkey*. Read the words at the bottom of the page and point out the /m/ sound in each one. The children can then work independently as they cut out and paste the words on the boxes to show what each monkey is doing.

 # Working with Words for /m/

1. The /m/ sound appears at the beginning of many sound patterns such as:

may	mat	map	mail	main	mow
my	mug	man	mop	more	mob
make	mine	mill	Mack	mink	mock

2. The /m/ is the final sound in many sound patterns, including *ame, am, im, um, one,* and *ime.* In your "Working with Words" activity, see whether the children can add some initial consonants to make new words. Direct the children's attention to the /m/ sound at the end of these newly formed words. Sample words are:

ame
came   flame   fame   name

am
ham   ma'am   Sam   Pam

Text copyright © Harry W. Forgan and James W. Forgan. Illustrations copyright © Pearson Learning.

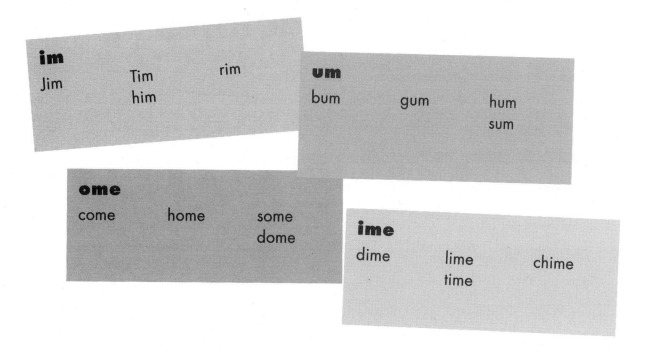

im
Jim   Tim   rim
him

um
bum   gum   hum
sum

ome
come   home   some
dome

ime
dime   lime   chime
time

3. The *m* can be combined with the letter *s* to form a consonant blend at the beginning of words, as in *small*, *smile*, and *smoke*. Additional words are provided in the lesson plan of the sound of *s*.

Hidden Pictures

map

marbles

mask

match

melon

mitten

money

monkey

mug

mushroom

Name_____ Date_____

Matching Monkeys

Directions: Match the monkeys with the words. Look at each monkey to find out what it is doing. Each monkey is doing something that sounds like the first sound in *monkey*. Listen as your teacher reads the words. Cut out each word and paste it by the monkey. Make a sentence using each word.

munching   mopping   mowing

marking   marching   missing

as in *nest*

Introducing /n/

1. Write the word *no* on the chalk-board. Ask the children what two sounds are in the word. They should point out /n/ and /ō/. Ask the children to name some other words that begin with /n/. If they have a difficult time thinking of words, you might give them some clues:

What I ask you to write on every paper (name)

An afternoon rest (nap)

The part of your body that is below your head (neck)

Something that is on your face (nose)

Something that squirrels like to eat (nuts)

Someone who helps take care of sick people (nurse)

Something adults like to read (newspaper)

If your papers are very nice, I say they are _____. (neat)

When we talk about trees, birds, flowers, and rain, we call these things _____. (nature)

The opposite of morning (night)

Go back over the words the children mentioned and emphasize the /n/ sound.

2. Once the children hear /n/ in the initial positions, you may want to write the word on the chalkboard. Have the children say the two sounds they hear in this word. Help them realize that they hear the /n/ at the end of the word. Ask them to think of other words that have /n/ at the end. Again, if they have difficulty, you might provide them with some clues, such as the following. Write the words on the board as the children answer the riddles.

Blows air to cool you	(fan)
You cook in it.	(pan)
Dogs like to chew it.	(bone)
You put a hot dog in it.	(bun)
You can write with it.	(pen)
The opposite of woman	(man)

You can put ice cream in it. (cone)

3. Now direct the children's attention to the list of hidden objects. Have them trace the letter *n* in each of the words as they say the names of the objects. Emphasize the /n/ as you show them the picture. As they find the objects in the hidden picture, they will again have an opportunity to say /n/.

Reinforcing /n/

Introduce the game "Naughty and Nice" by writing the word *naughty* on the board. Read it to the children and ask them for a word that begins with /n/ and means the opposite of *naughty.* Tell the children that the name of the game they are going to play is "Naughty and Nice." As you show the children the game board, help them read all the words that begin with /n/. Point out that if they land on a space that says "naughty!" they will be moving back. If they land on a space with the word "nice!", they will get to move ahead. To win the game, they must throw the number on the die that will move them exactly the right number of spaces to land on "Nice job! You've won."

Working with Words for the Sound of /n/

1. The sound /n/ is found at the beginning of many sound patterns:

Nick	nag	need	nest
not	nay	nip	nab
now	nap	new	nail
night	nill	nack	nine

2. Since there are many sound patterns that have /n/ in the final position, you may want to use these in your "Working with Words" activity.

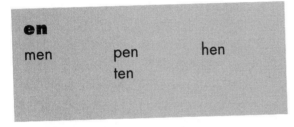

en

| men | pen | hen |
| | ten | |

un

| bun | sun | run |
| | | fun |

ain

| brain | chain | drain |
| | | grain |

ine

| line | mine | pine |

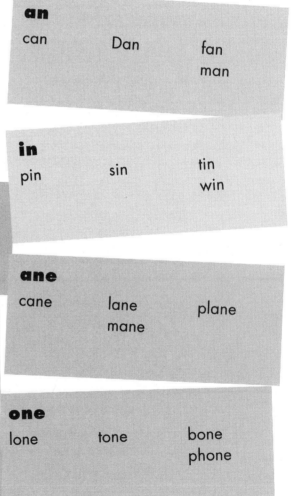

an

| can | Dan | fan |
| | | man |

in

| pin | sin | tin |
| | | win |

ane

| cane | lane | plane |
| | mane | |

one

| lone | tone | bone |
| | | phone |

3. The sound of /n/ can be combined with some other letters to form consonant blends. The *sn* combination is common at the beginning of words, as in *snake, snack,* and *snow.* Additional words are presented in the lesson plan for the sound of *s.* The letter *n* can also be blended with *d* and *t* at the end of words to make the consonant blends /nd/ and /nt/, as in the following words. Use these words to help children see and hear the blends. Have the children notice the sound patterns.

nt

ant	spent	tent
plant	can't	pants
mint	bent	sent

nd

and	find	grind
sand	band	grand
send	bend	friend
kind	spend	blind

Hidden Pictures

needle
nest
net
nickel

nose
notebook
nurse
nut

146

Name_____ Date_____

Naughty and Nice

Directions: Two players can play this game. Each player should put a token on Start. The idea is to move all the way around the letter *N* to the space that says "Nice job! You've won!" Take turns throwing a die. If you land on a space that says "Naughty!", you will be moving back. If you land on a space that says "Nice!", you will get to move ahead. You must land on the space that says "Nice job!" with the exact count to win. Be *nice*, not *naughty*, as you play this game!

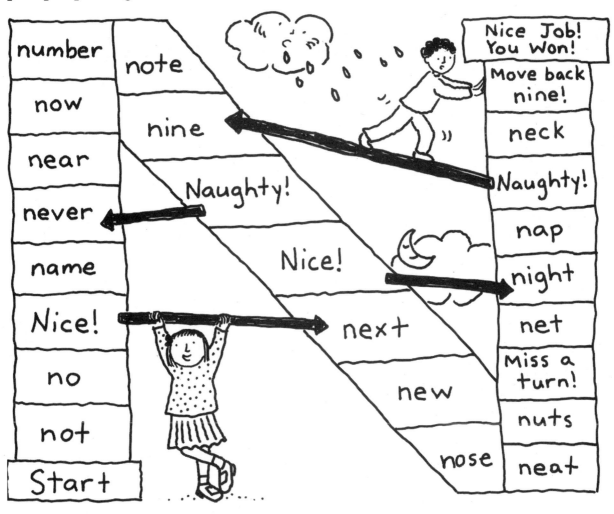

ng
as in *ring*

 ## Introducing /ng/

1. Give the children the hidden objects picture. Say that all of the hidden objects have the /ng/ sound. Direct their attention to the list of objects with /ng/.

2. After they have found the objects in the picture, see if they can tell you any other words that have the /ng/ sound. Perhaps they will suggest such words as *king, song, hung, sang, rang, hang, swing, sling,* and *tongue.* If not, you can say some of these words so they can hear the /ng/. Write these words for the children so that they begin to associate *ng* and /ng/.

Reinforcing /ng/

Give each child a copy of the "Sing" activity. They can work in pairs or individually to write a rap or song using as many words as they can with the /ng/ sound. Read the words in the word box aloud with the class, and encourage students to use other words they know with the /ng/ sound. Allow children to recite their rap or song to the class when finished.

Working with Words for /ng/

1. You always teach /ng/ in the final position of a word or syllable. You can teach *ing* as a sound pattern, since this combination of sounds is frequent. Use these words to teach students the sound /ng/.

bring	sting	working	having
king	thing	talking	wanting
sing	swing	walking	swimming
string	ping	singing	watching
song	hung		
long	rung		
wrong	young		
strong	hunger		

Hidden Pictures

fang
finger
gong
hanger
jingle bells
Ping-Pong ball
ring
sling
string
wing

Name_____ Date_____

Sing

Directions: Use as many words with the /ng/ sound as you can to write a rap or song on the back of this sheet. Sing your rap or song to the class when you are finished.

Sample

One day in the spring I saw a king.

He was singing and rocking in a swing.

We started talking and he kept rocking.

Time flew by then I had to start walking.

fang	bring	long	lung	swing	talking
sang	king	song	hung	wing	walking
rang	sting	strong	sprung	ring	singing
hang	thing	wrong	young	string	watching

ŏ
as in *octopus*

Introducing /ŏ/

1. Draw a simple outline of an octopus on the chalkboard. In the center of the octopus, write the word *octopus*. On each of the arms write a short *o* word. You may want to use the following: *dog, log, clock, top, lock, mop, rock,* and *frog.*

2. Tell the children this octopus was hungry and was able to catch lots of things with his arms. Ask them to listen as you read what the octopus caught. After the children have heard the words, ask them what

sound all of the words have. If they are not able to tell you, tell them it is the same sound they hear at the beginning of *octopus*. Say each word again and have the children repeat them to hear the /ŏ/ sound.

3. Tell the children all of the hidden objects also have the short *o* sound. Direct their attention to these objects and then have them find them in the picture. As they find the different objects, have them emphasize the /ŏ/ sound.

Reinforcing /ŏ/

Children play the game "Hop or Stop" to reinforce the /ŏ/ sound. Divide the class into cooperative groups of four, and distribute the game board and tokens. Before playing, you or the students should write /ŏ/ words on blank index cards. Make three cards with STOP (each group needs about 15 cards). Instruct children to place the cards facedown and to take turns drawing a card. If a child can read the word with the /ŏ/ sound, he or she hops one space forward. If a child draws a STOP card, he or she goes back and starts over. The first student to successfully hop to the middle is the winner. Words with /ŏ/ are: *shop, stop, top, crop, drop, mop, pop, rooftop, shortstop, dock, rock, off, jog, hog, frog, fog, October, odd, on, hot, pot, copy, job, not, dot.*

Working with Words for the Sound of /ŏ/

Help the children realize the vowel sound is usually short when a word has the CVC pattern. You might want to list words such as the following and have them notice the consonant at the end. Tell the children that when they come to a word that has an o, they should try the short o sound if the syllable ends in a consonant. You can teach common sound patterns containing /ŏ/ during the "Working with Words" activity. Use these words:

ob

Bob	lob	mob
knob	cob	sob
	job	

ock

block	sock	mock
clock	dock	flock
lock	knock	smock
rock		

ŏ

og
dog   hog   jog
fog   log   clog
       frog

ond
blond   fond   bond
         pond   beyond

ong
long   song   wrong
        strong   oblong

op
chop   hop   pop
cop   mop   stop
drop   crop   top
        shop   flop

ot
cot   shot   rot
dot   jot   spot
hot   knot   clot
pot   not   plot
       got   trot
       lot

Hidden Pictures

block · clock · dog · frog · log · octopus · sock · top

Ŏ

Text copyright © Harry W. Forgan and James W. Forgan. Illustrations copyright © Pearson Learning.

155

Hop or Stop

Directions: Place the cards facedown. Draw a card. If you can read the word with the /ŏ/ sound, hop one space forward. If you draw a STOP card, go back to Start. The first one to hop to the middle is the winner.

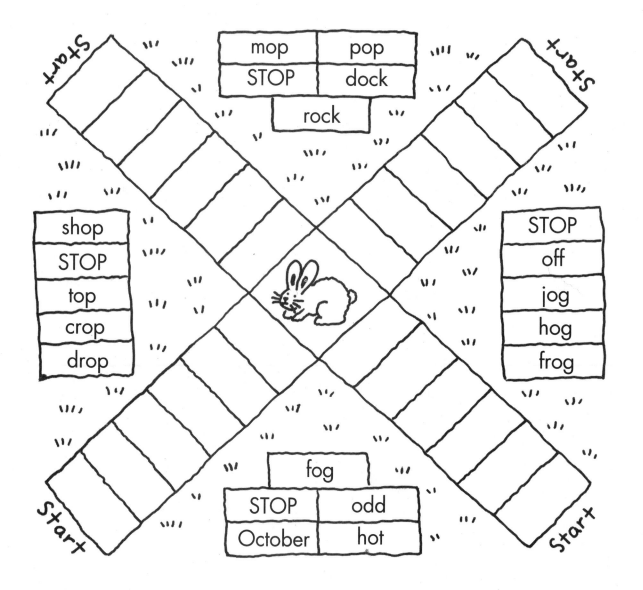

as in *bone*

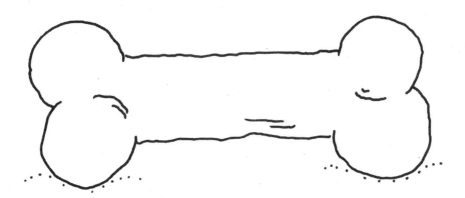

 ## Introducing /ō/

1. Tell the children that you are going to sing the first line of some of your favorite songs. Ask them to listen to the first sound they hear in each line, since that is the sound they are going to learn today. Sing the following first lines:

Old McDonald had a farm.

Oh, say can you see.

Over hill, over dale, we will hit the dusty trail.

Oh, give me a home where the buffalo roam.

2. Ask the children to tell you what sound they heard. You can tell them this is the long sound of *o*, because it sounds like the name of the letter *o*.

3. Show the children the list of the hidden objects. As they identify the objects, have them isolate the long *o* sound. Now they can find the hidden objects in the picture.

4. After the children have found the objects, ask them whether they can think of any other words that have the long *o* sound. If not, you can write some: *told, hope, gold, fold, boat, home, roll,* and *rope.* Give the children an opportunity to say the words. Tell them that if they hear you say any more words today with the /ō/ sound, they should remember them and you will give them a treat. Give Life Savers™ (the shape of o) to the children who hear words with the /ō/ sound. Write the words on the board for the children to read, then give all of the children Life Savers.

Reinforcing /ō/

Give each student a copy of the "Overflow" handout and read the words aloud as a class. Instruct students to reread each word and find the /ō/ sound words. Students write the /ō/ sound words along the riverbank to help stop the river from overflowing.

Working with Words for /ō/

1. In nearly all words with the *oa* combination, the *o* is long and the *a* is silent. You can use the following words to teach or reinforce this principle:

oat

| oat | boat | float |
| | coat | throat |

oad

| load | road | toad |

oa

coach	croak	foam
soak	coal	roast
	goal	toast

2. Review the silent *e* principle (in a syllable or word with two vowels one of which is a final *e*, the final *e* is usually silent and the other vowel is long). Use the following words.

oke

broke	poke	choke
joke	woke	smoke
	stroke	spoke

one

bone	lone	phone
cone	tone	shone
	zone	stone

ole

hole	pole	stole
mole	role	whole

ope

cope	mope	rope
dope	nope	scope
hope	Pope	slope

ose

hose	pose	close
nose	rose	prose
	chose	those

ove

cove	wove	drove
	clove	stove

3. The children will soon learn that sometimes *o* and *w* combine to make the /ow/ sound, as in *cow*. This is true for about half the words that have the *ow* combination. In other words with the *ow* combination, the *ow* is pronounced /ō/. When you begin to teach the *ow* diphthong, tell the children they can try either the /ō/ sound or the /ow/ sound, and then see whether the word makes sense in the context. Words with /ō/ spelled *ow* are:

crow	show	throw
grow	own	glow
slow	bowl	mow
bow	know	low
blow	flow	shown
know		
snow		

Hidden Pictures

boat
bone
coat
goat
pole

pony
rope
rose
soap
toe

ō

160

Text copyright © Harry W. Forgan and James W. Forgan. Illustrations copyright © Pearson Learning.

Overflow!!

Directions: Help stop the river from overflowing by writing the words with /ō/ along the shore.

opposites	ox	no	zero	boat
go	slow	box	on	note
oak	obey	oat	joke	
road	pot	home	show	
ocean	odd	body	Ohio	
coast	toad	slow	pot	

ôr
as in *fork*

 # Introducing /ôr/

1. Begin this lesson by holding up a paper bag containing an orange, an Oreo™ cookie, or a picture of an organ. Tell the children to guess what you have in the bag. After a few guesses, they will need some clues. Tell them that it begins with the letter *o* and that the next letter is *r*, so it sounds like /ôr/ at the beginning. If the children do not arrive at the correct answer, show them what is in the bag and then write the words on the board.

2. Write other words having the /ôr/ sound, such as *or, orchestra, ornament,* and *orphan.* Have the chil-

dren say these words after you. Now write the words that have /ôr/ in the middle or final position, such as *for, store, fork, horn,* and *floor.* Tell the children that usually when *o* is in front of an *r*, the bossy *r* tells it to say /ôr/. Read the words and have the children read them after you, to say and hear /ôr/.

3. Now direct the children's attention to the list of the hidden objects. Have them trace the /ôr/ combination as they say the words. Ask the children to find the hidden objects and suggest other words that contain this sound. Use all the words in sentences.

Reinforcing /ôr/

Introduce the game "Roar or Snore" by telling the children they are now going to play a "quiet" game. This is a "quiet" game because they do not want to wake up the lion and make him roar. They want the lion to snore. Have the children cut out all the words on the sheet and place them in a paper bag. Each child puts a token in the center position on the lion and decides what

number he or she is going to be. Tell the children to take turns reaching into the paper bag and pulling out a word. If a child pulls out a word other than *roar* and can read it and use the word in a sentence, he or she gets to move forward one place toward Score. If he or she pulls out the word *roar*, the child must go back to the lion. The first one to reach Score is the winner.

Working with Words for /ôr/

1. Many times *ore* is a sound pattern as in the words:

more	sore	score
store	tore	wore
core	fore	pore
chore	shore	swore

2. Additional words to use in "Working with Words" activities to teach /ôr/ are:

north	forest	forty	boarder
horse	horn	morning	chorus
oral	before	more	order
thorn	coral	report	accord
story	form	fort	force
cork	storm	fork	born
pork	torn		

Hidden Pictures

cord		horn	
core		horse	
corn		oar	
door		orange	
fork		sword	

Name_____ Date_____

Roar or Snore

Directions: See if you can get out of the lion's cage while he is snoring. Cut out the words on the page. Put them in a paper bag. Decide what number you will be and place your token on the lion. Take turns reaching into the bag to get a word. If you are able to read the word and use it in a sentence, you get to move one space toward Score. If you draw the word *roar*, you must go back to the lion. The first one to reach Score is the winner.

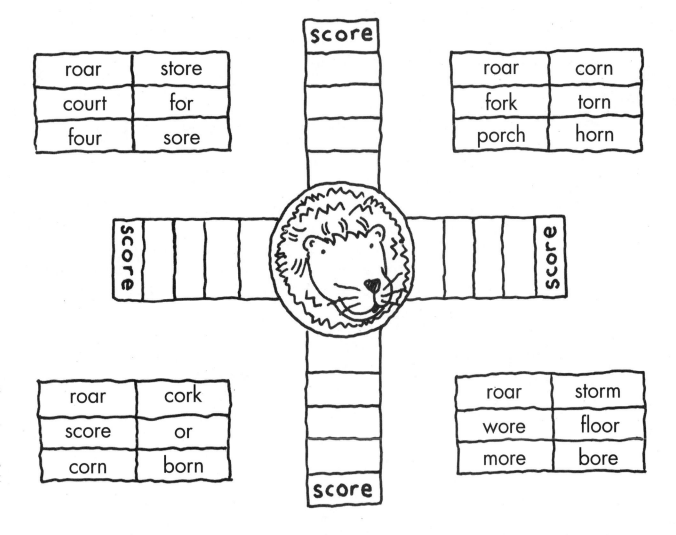

roar	store
court	for
four	sore

roar	corn
fork	torn
porch	horn

score

score

score

roar	cork
score	or
corn	born

roar	storm
wore	floor
more	bore

score

ou

as in *owl*

 **Introducing the ou-ow Diphthong**

1. Ask the children what they say when they get hurt. They will probably say, "ouch." Write the word *ouch* on the board and tell them that the first part of this word is one of the vowel sounds. It sounds like /ou/, as in *blouse, house, mouth, our, cloud,* and *couch.*

2. Write the words on the board so the children can see the *ou* combination. Tell them that two other letters can also make this sound: /ow/.

Write these words on the board: *cow, owl, clown, wow, now,* and *how.* Read them for the children so they can hear the /ou/ sound. Now have the children read the words with you so they can say /ou/.

3. Tell the children all of the objects in the hidden picture have the /ou/ sound. Have the children say the words on the list of hidden objects and trace the *ou* or *ow.* As they find the objects in the picture, have them emphasize the /ou/ sound.

Reinforcing the *ou-ow* Diphthong

Ask the children whether they have ever pounded nails. Ask them what they say if they are pounding nails and hit their thumbs. Tell them that today they get to pound some nails and say /ou/ in a game called "Pound Down!" Ask them what vowel sound they hear in *pound* and *down*. Tell them that the object of the game is to see how many nails they can pound down by unscrambling the letters. If they are able to unscramble the letters to make a word with the /ou/ sound, as in *pound down*, they have pounded the nail down into the wood. Tell them they can check their scores at the bottom of the reinforcement activity page. After they have unscrambled the words, have the children pronounce them again to hear /ou/ and realize that it is spelled with *ou* or *ow*. Have children use each word in a sentence.

Working with Words for the *ou-ow* Diphthong

1. The children probably remember that the *ow* combination makes the long *o* sound, as in *row, low, grow, mow,* and *tow*. Tell them that they will have to read the rest of the sentence to see whether *ow* should be pronounced /o/ or /ou/ when they are in doubt. You can use these sentences to help them understand this technique:

The car had to be *towed*.

Cows give milk.

Now is the time to go.

Farmers *plow* the soil.

We all laughed at the *clown*.

The crops will *grow*.

Have the children substitute the /ō/ sound in each of the above *ow* words and lead them to realize how the context will tell them whether a word contains long *o* or the diphthong *ow*. Phonograms to use in

teaching the *ow* spelling of /ou/ are:

owl

fowl   howl   growl
                scowl

ow

bow   now   chow
cow   sow   plow
how   vow   prow
        brow   bow-wow

own

down   town   crown
gown   brown   drown
        clown   frown

2. You can use these examples to extend the knowledge of the *ou*

spelling of /ou/ in the "Working with Words" activities:

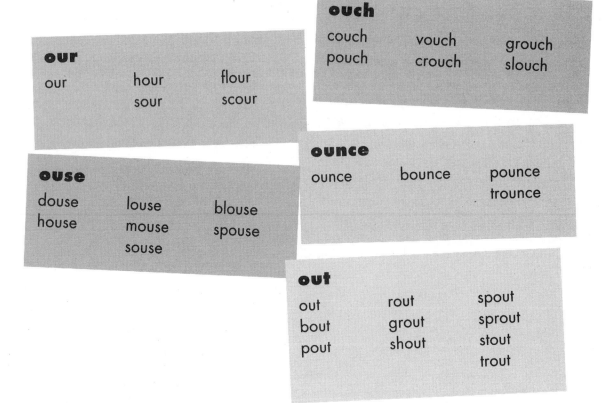

our

our   hour   flour
        sour   scour

ouch

couch   vouch   grouch
pouch   crouch   slouch

ouse

douse   louse   blouse
house   mouse   spouse
        souse

ounce

ounce   bounce pounce
                trounce

out

out   rout   spout
bout   grout   sprout
pout   shout   stout
                trout

Hidden Pictures

clown    mouth

crown

flower

mouse   owl   towel   tower

Reinforcement Activity for /ou/

Name_____ Date_____

Pound Down!

Directions: See how many nails you can pound down. To pound down a nail, you must unscramble the letters to make a word with the vowel sound as in *pound* or *down*. Check your score at the bottom of the page.

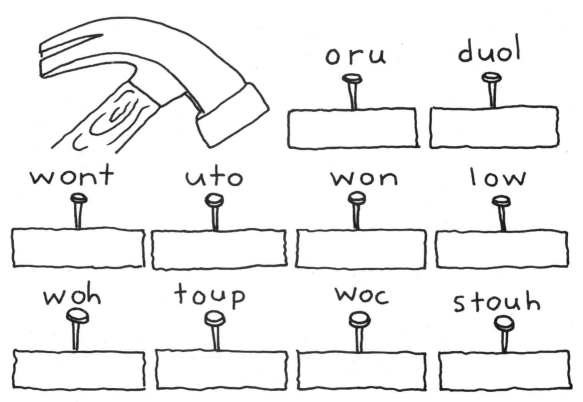

oru   duol

wont   uto   won   low

woh   toup   woc   stouh

Scoring Guide

9–10	Wow! You did not have to say, "ouch"!
7–8	Pretty good. You should be proud!
5–6	About Average
3–4	You were just clowning around.
1–2	Ouch! Better pick up your thumb off the ground!

oi
as in *oil*

Introducing the *oi-oy* Diphthong

1. Introduce the *oi-oy* diphthong by telling the children to listen as you say the following words. Ask them to listen to see what vowel sound they hear. Say "*boy, joy, toy, oil, point, noise,* and *spoil*." If the children are unable to tell you /oi/, say the sound, and again have them listen as you read the words. Write the words on the board so the children can see that /oi/ is spelled either *oi* or *oy*. Have the children say each word again and feel the glide of the two letters.

2. Ask them what farm animal makes the /oi/ sound (the hog—oink). Tell them the hidden objects all have the /oi/ sound, as in *oink*. Direct their attention to the list of the hidden objects and again have them notice the *oi* or *oy* spelling of each word. Tell the children that when they see a word that has *oi* or *oy*, they should say /oi/. Now have fun finding the items in the hidden objects picture, and use each word in a sentence.

Reinforcing the oi-oy Diphthong

Tell the children that Joy wants to oil her bike. The bike needs six drops of oil. Ask the children to see whether they can help Joy by writing a word that has the /oi/ sound (*coin, soil, oil, royal, spoil, joy, noise, toy*) on each drop of oil. When they have six words with the /oi/ sound, the bike is oiled and there will not be any noise. Tell the children they can get clues to words with the /oi/ sound by looking at the letters on the oil can. After the children have completed this activity, have them read their words and again notice the /oi/ sound and the two ways that it can be spelled.

Working with Words for the Sound of the *oi-oy* Diphthong

1. For the "Working with Words" activity for /oi/, you might use these words (if they are in children's listening vocabularies):

oin

coin	join	loin
		groin

oil

oil	coil	toil
boil	foil	spoil
	soil	broil

oy

boy	joy	soy
coy	roy	toy
		ploy

2. Other words might include:

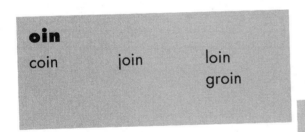

moist	voice
poison	destroy
point	noise
poise	avoid
choice	employ

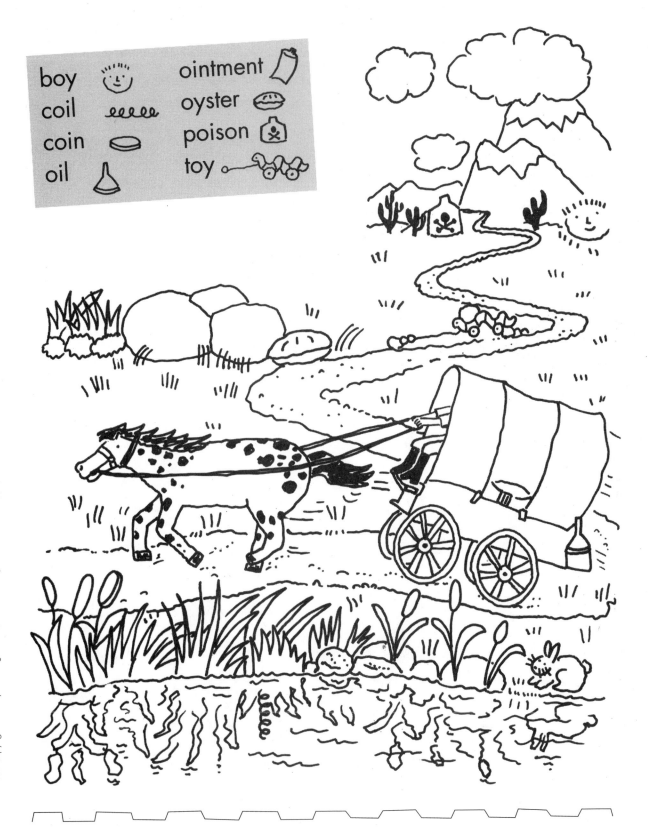

oi

Hidden Pictures

boy
coil
coin
oil
ointment
oyster
poison
toy

R E I N F O R C E M E N T   A c t i v i t y   f o r   / o i /

Name_____   Date_____

Oil the Bike

Directions: Joy needs to oil her bike to get rid of the noise. She will need six drops of oil. You can help her by writing a word with /oi/ on each drop. Clues to words that have the *oi* or *oy* spelling of /oi/ can be found in the hidden words on the oilcan.

174

as in *spoon*

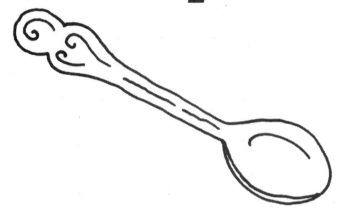

■ ■

Introducing /o͞o/

1. Ask the children what sound they make when they see a picture of something sad or tragic. Many people make the long *oo* sound when they want to express sympathy or sadness. If the children in your class do not respond with /o͞o/, as in *cool*, *zoo*, or *fool*, tell them that many people say /o͞o/.

2. Tell them you have some words that have the long *oo* sound in them. Write the word *cool* on the board. Say the word for the children so they can hear the /o͞o/ sound in the middle position. Now erase the *c* and add *f*; see whether the children can tell you the word *fool*.

3. Repeat this procedure with *t* for *tool*, *p* for *pool*, *sch* for *school*, and *sp* for *spool*. Tell the children that when they see a word that has *oo* and ends in *l*, they should say the long *oo* sound.

4. Explain that the long double-*o* sound does not sound like the name of the letter *o*. This is a new sound, different from /ō/. Mention the fact that *oo* can also be short, as in *book* and *look*. Point out the difference between /o͝o/ and /o͞o/ and tell the children that today you will work on /o͞o/.

5. Now refer the children to the list of hidden objects; have them notice the /o͞o/ sound and the different ways that it can be spelled. As they find the hidden objects, have the children emphasize the /o͞o/ sound.

Reinforcing /o͞o/

Give children the activity page, "Noodle the Poodle." Tell the children that Noodle the poodle followed the children to school. The principal told her to go home. She needs to find her way home but can only go on the path with the words having /o͞o/, as in her name, Noodle. The children should find the path that Noodle took home. If they come to a word with the short oo sound, as in *book*, they must change direction, because Noodle can only walk on long *oo* words. After the children have completed this puzzle, have them read the words with /o͞o/. The children should read *cool, spoon, moon, loop, hoop, goose, boot, spool, choose, spook, noon, broom, groom, boo, zoo, food, room,* and *soon.*

Working with Words for /o͞o/

1. Use these phonograms to teach children /o͞o/:

ood

shoo   food   mood

oo

boo   goo   too
coo   moo   zoo

oof

goof   proof   spoof
roof

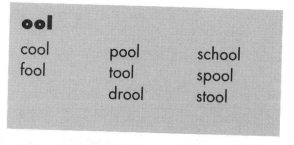

oom

boom	room	broom
doom	zoom	gloom
loom	bloom	groom

ool

cool	pool	school
fool	tool	spool
	drool	stool

oon

| coon | noon | spoon |
| moon | soon | |

oop

coop	loop	stoop
hoop	droop	swoop
	scoop	troop

oose

| goose | loose | moose |
| noose | | |

oot

boot	loot	scoot
hoot	root	shoot
	toot	

2. Since /ōō/ is more common than /ŏŏ/, you may want to tell the children that when they come to a word with *oo* and they are not sure what sound it represents, they should try /ōō/, as in *boo*, before they try /ŏŏ/, as in *book*. Other words representing /ōō/ include:

soup	group
snooze	lose
whose	booth
tooth	rooster
balloon	cartoon
moose	

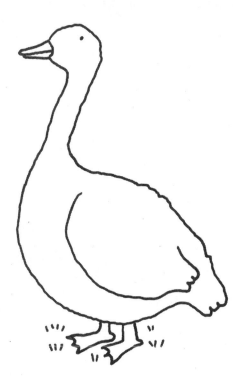

Hidden Pictures

boot
broom
moon
rooster
soup

spook
spool
spoon
stool
tool

Name_____ Date_____

Noodle the Poodle

Directions: Noodle the poodle followed the children to school one day. The principal told her, "Go home!" Noodle is having a hard time finding the right path to take home. She can only go on the long *oo* words that have the same sounds as in her name. When she comes to a word with a short *oo* sound as in *book*, she has to change her direction. See if you can draw a line to show the path Noodle should use to get home.

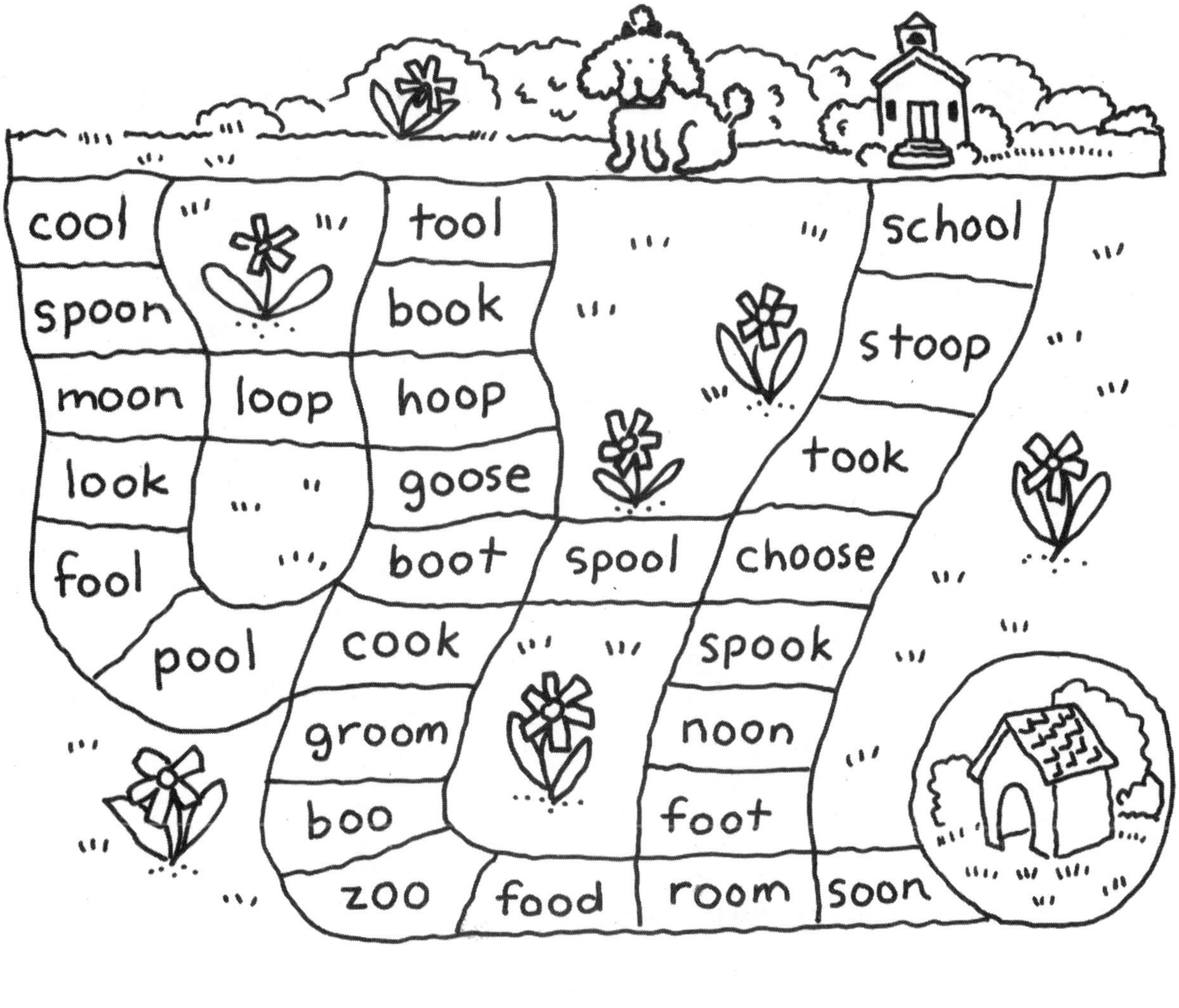

179

as in *book*

 ## Introducing /ŏŏ/

1. Write the word *look* on the board. Tell the children the vowel sound in look is /ŏŏ/. You may want to review the sound of /ōō/, and tell the children that another sound *o* can make is /ŏŏ/, as in *book*, *cook*, *took*, and *hook*. Contrast the sounds so the children can hear the different sounds represented by *oo*.

2. Now read the following story. When they hear /ŏŏ/, as in *look*, the children should clap. When they clap, write the word on the board. Read this story.

Tom *put* on his *hood*. He got his *books*. His mom said, "Remember to *look* both ways before crossing the street." He *took* her advice. A guard *stood* at the crossing. He reminded Tom that he *should* hurry. But Tom *could* not. He was thinking about the homework that he *should* have done. Finally, he reached the school and *pulled* the door open. He *put* his books on his desk because it was too *full* inside. *Wouldn't* you know, someone stepped on his *foot*. It was the *bully* of the class. Tom *could* have hit him, but the teacher was *looking*. Instead, he just smiled and said, "*Good* morning." This really *shook* the *bully*. Now they would be friends.

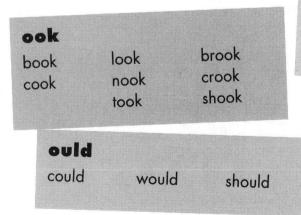

3. You have listed many words with /o͝o/ on the board. Do not be concerned if the children did not identify each word, but rather use the words you have to help the children hear the /o͝o/ sound. Have them repeat the words after you so they get a chance to say the /o͝o/. Now direct their attention to the list of hidden objects; have them listen to the /o͝o/ and notice the o. As they find the objects in the picture, they should try to emphasize the short oo sound.

Reinforcing /o͝o/

Give each child a copy of "Cookie Clues" and read aloud each word inside a cookie. Tell students to complete the sentences using one word from each cookie. After children finish, have them read their sentences aloud to a partner.

Working with Words for /o͝o/

Use these phonograms to teach the sound of /o͝o/:

ook

book	look	brook
cook	nook	crook
	took	shook

ood

| good | hood | wood |
| | | stood |

ould

| could | would | should |

oot

| foot | soot |

Hidden Pictures

book
cookie
crook
foot

football
hood
hook
wood

Name_____ Date_____

Cookie Clues

Directions: Use one word from each cookie to complete the sentences.

1. We _ _ _ _ a trip to the Grand Canyon.
2. I like to _ _ _ _ eggs.
3. My _ _ _ _ is sore.
4. The policeman caught the _ _ _ _ _.
5. I am reading a good _ _ _ _.
6. _ _ _ _ _ _ _ _ is my favorite sport.
7. I caught the fish with a _ _ _ _ and line.
8. We put _ _ _ _ in our fireplace.
9. " _ _ _ _ catch," yelled the coach.
10. My blanket is made from _ _ _ _.
11. Our pool is _ _ _ _ of water.
12. Please don't _ _ _ _ my hair.
13. The _ _ _ _ was running loose in the street.
14. I _ _ _ _ _ _ like to go to the movie.
15. We _ _ _ _ _ _ wash the car.

p

as in *pig*

Introducing /p/

1. Introduce /p/ by telling the children you see many things in the classroom that begin with /p/. Say "*paper, pencils, pens, pair of scissors, pants, pets, pennies, pins,* and *people*" Ask the children to tell you what sound they heard at the beginning of all the words you said.

2. Tell the children there is one thing you forgot to mention that also begins with /p/, and it wants to talk with them today. Show them one of the puppets you have available in the room. Have the puppet say some words. If the words begin with

/p/, the children should stand up and wave at the puppet. If the words do not begin with /p/, the children should remain seated and say /p/, /p/, /p/. Use the following words: *baby, puppy, puzzle, cat, hair, lamb, paddle, papa, pop, parachute, money, porch, puddle, book, pizza, pinch, cold,* and *goat.*

3. Show them the list of the hidden objects. Go over the items and then direct the children to find them in the picture, again emphasizing the /p/.

Reinforcing /p/

Tell the children you are going to give each one of them a pocket and you want them to put all of the pictures of things that begin with /p/ into the pocket. The pictures that do not begin with /p/ should not be pasted on the pocket. Hand out the activity, "What's in Your Pocket?" The children will cut out the pictures of a pin, parachute, puzzle,

penny, pan, pen, pig, and pepper, and glue them on the pocket. After the children have completed the project, ask them what items are in the pocket. Again have them notice that all of the objects they pasted on the pocket begin with /p/. Write the words on the board so the children can associate *p* with /p/.

Working with Words for /p/

1. Use these words to teach children the sound /p/ in the initial position:

pack pass police pick pan pine

page path pile pot pest

pain pay perfect pail pink

pants pull push pop pat

pill Pam pin pout pew

2. The /p/ sound is heard in the final position in many words, especially in the sound patterns of *ap*, *ip*, and *op*. Use the following words to teach /p/ in the final position.

ap

clap	cap	slap
flap	map	snap
lap	nap	strap
	wrap	tap
		trap

ape

| ape | grape | shape |
| | tape | |

ip

chip	grip	sip
clip	hip	skip
dip	lip	slip
drip	nip	strip
flip	rip	tip
trip	whip	zip

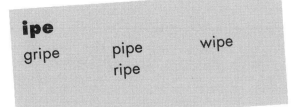

ipe

gripe   pipe   wipe
         ripe

op

chop	flop	prop
cop	hop	shop
drop	mop	slop
crop	plop	stop
	pop	top

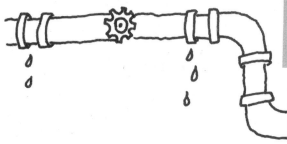

3. The letter *p* forms consonant blends in the initial position with the letters *l* or *r*. Words you can use in helping the children learn the *pl* and *pr* combinations follow.

pl

place	plane	plan
plaza	planet	plant
plaster	plastic	plate
play	please	plenty
pliers	plow	plug
plumber	plump	plus
plain	plank	

pr

practice	praise	prayer
prescription	present	press
pretzel	prevent	price
primer	print	prison
product	program	promise
preach	prepare	
pretend	pretty	
pride	primary	
prize	problem	
protect	proud	

Hidden Pictures

package | pie
paintbrush | pig
paw | pin
peanut | pipe
pencil | pizza
penny | pumpkin

Name_____ Date_____

What's in Your Pocket?

Directions: Look at the picture below. If a picture begins with /p/, as in *pocket*, cut it out and paste it on the pocket. If the picture does not begin with /p/, do not put in on the pocket.

q

= /kw/, as in *queen*

Introducing the /kw/ Sound of *q*

1. Tell the children there is one letter of the alphabet that is always with another letter. Write the letter *q* on the board and tell the children the letter *q* is always followed by *u*. Explain to the children that when they see *q* and *u* together they will be saying /kw/, because *q* does not have its own sound.

2. Ask the children to listen and look as you say and write these words so they can hear the /kw/: *queen, question, quick, quiet, quit, quote, quite,* and *quiz.* Now have the children repeat these words after you so

they have an opportunity to say /kw/. They may realize that /kw/ is actually a blend of /k/ and /w/.

3. Direct children's attention to the list of hidden objects. Have them notice that each word has the letter combination *qu*; however, some words begin with *s.* Point out that *squ* is a three-letter consonant blend (/skw/), as heard in *squirrel, squad, square, squirt, squeak,* and *squeeze.* As the children find the hidden objects, have them emphasize the /kw/ or /skw/ sound.

Reinforcing the /kw/ Sound of q

To reinforce /kw/ and /skw/ sounds, tell children they will play "Tic-Tac-Quack." Divide the class into groups of two. Tell students "Tic-Tac-Quack" is played just like "Tic-Tac-Toe" except instead of using Xs and Os, they use words with the /kw/ and /skw/ sounds. Begin by handing out the activity page. Then read aloud all the words in the word box. Next, one student uses the /kw/ words and another uses the words beginning with /skw/ to try and get three in a row. The first person to get three in a row says, "Quack."

Working with Words for the /kw/ Sound of *q* and the /skw/ Sound of *squ*

1. Words to use in your "Working with Words" activity in which *qu* represents /kw/ or *squ* represents /skw/ are:

quack	quad
qualify	quarrel
quiz	quail
quiver	earthquake
squeal	request
quotient	quota
quote	

Hidden Pictures

quart
quarter
queen
question
mark

square
squash
squaw
squirrel

Lemonade
5¢

Name_____ Date_____

Tic-Tac-Quack

Directions: Play "Tic-Tac-Quack" just like "Tic-Tac-Toe," except instead of using Xs and Os, you use words with the /kw/ or /skw/ sounds. First read aloud all the words in the word box. Next, one student uses the /kw/ words and the other uses the words beginning with /skw/ to try and get three in a row. Write a different word in each square. The first person to get three in a row says, "Quack."

/kw/ sound		/skw/ sound	
question	queen	squeak	squid
quilt	quick	squirrel	squirt gun
quack	quake	square	squat
quarrel	quit	squeeze	squirt
quiz	quiet	squeal	squash

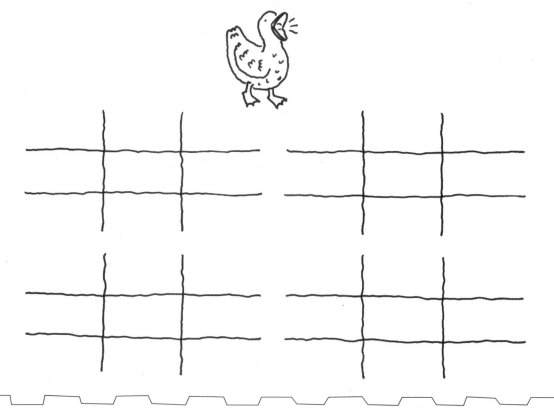

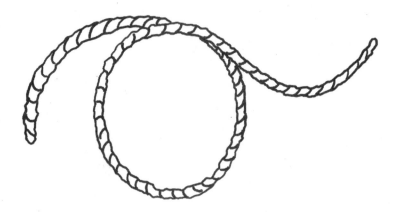

r
as in *rope*

Introducing /r/

1. Introduce this sound by beginning with the list of hidden objects. Have the children name the objects: *rabbit, radio, raft, raisin, rake, rattle, record, ring, rock,* and *rope*. After the children have mentioned each object, have them indicate what sound they hear at the beginning of each word. Now direct the children to find the hidden objects in the picture. After the children have found the objects, review the /r/ sound.

2. Tell the children you would like to play "Red Rover" with them. Ask them how both of the words in this game begin. Write "Red Rover" on the board, pointing out the *r*s as you say the sounds. Divide the children into two equal teams and have one team begin by saying, "Red Rover, Red Rover, let _____ come over." If the child whose name was called is able to say a word that begins with /r/, he or she does not have to go over to the other team. If he of she cannot say a word within ten seconds, he or she joins the other team. The team with more players at the end of any given amount of time is the winner.

3. You may want to make a rule that children must use a different word beginning with /r/ each time, to make the game more challenging and to expose the children to many words with the sound of *r*. Write the words on the chalkboard so the children make the sound–symbol association.

Reinforcing /r/

Use the game "Ringo," played like "Bingo," to reinforce the /r/ sound. Use 24 words with the /r/ sound from your Red Rover activity or select 24 words from "Working with Words."

Hand out the activity, and instruct the children to write one word in each box. Give each student a strip of colored paper to tear into markers.

Working with Words for /r/

1. Words you can use in your "Working with Words" activity to help children learn /r/ are as follows:

reach	rat	rose	roll	rag
read	red	roof	railroad	real
recess	run	round	ran	race

2. The letter *r* is part of many consonant blends. *R* can be combined with *b, c, d, f, g, p, t, st,* and *th* to make either a two- or three-letter blend, as in *bring, cry, dry, fry, gray, pray, tree, street,* and *three.* Additional words are provided for each of the above blends in the lesson plans for the first letter of each blend. For example, turn to the section on the sound of *b* for words that begin with the /br/ blend.

Hidden Pictures

rabbit
radio
raft
raisin
rake

rattle
record
ring
rock
rope

Name_____ Date_____

Ringo

Directions: Write one word with the /r/ sound in each box. Listen for your teacher to call a word. Place a marker over the word.

R	I	N	G	O
		FREE		

S
as in *sun*

 ## Introducing /s/

1. Tell the children that today they are going to play "Simon Says." Review the directions by reminding the children they should only do as you say if you say "Simon Says" first. Each time you give a direction, write the words that begin with /s/. You can use these directions:

Simon says "sit."

Stand.

Simon says "salute."

Simon says "sing."

Simon says "saw."

Put your right hand up.

Simon says "be silent."

Simon says "sigh."

Simon says "sit down."

2. After the game, have the children notice your list of words on the board. Ask them what sound they hear at the beginning of the words. Ask the children what sound the letter *s* makes. You might want to ask what animal makes that sound. The children will probably suggest a snake. If not, you can mention it.

3. Show the children the list of the hidden objects. Have the children notice the /s/. You might also have the children realize that the letter *s* looks like a snake, and that /s/ is the sound a snake makes. Tell the children that today they are going to be detectives, helping one of their classmates find the hidden pictures in the classroom. Give each child a picture and again have them notice the /s/ sound as they find the hidden objects.

Reinforcing /s/

Give each student a copy of the reinforcement activity. Students can work in pairs or independently to make at least 10 smaller words from the big word *supercalifragilisticexpialidocious.*

Give students the opportunity to share one word they made from the big word. Sample words include *slip, sip,* and *spill.*

Working with Words for /s/

1. Words you can use in teaching /s/ are:

say	sack	sad	sank
so	such	salt	see
sip	sister	soon	same
sat	sale	simple	set
side	some	sick	sell
seem	sing	seed	
say	sail	sin	
soft	sink	sob	

son	sock	suck	sight
sunk	Sam	sum	sag
sack	sank		

2. The letter *s* can be blended with many letters to form a two- or three-letter consonant blend. You can use the following word lists during "Working with Words" as you help the children develop a knowledge of the consonant blends. Help the children realize they should say only one sound when they see these consonant combinations in words.

scr

scrape
scratch

screen
screw

scribble
scrub

sc/sch

scab
scalp
scale

scarf
schedule
school

scold
scooter
score
scout

sl

slack
slant
sleep
slice

slick
cling
clow
slam
slave

sled
slide
slip
slop
slush

sk

skate
sketch
skid
skip
skull

sky
brisk
mask
skeleton
ski
skin

skirt
skunk
risk
ask
dusk

sn

snake
snap
sneak

snicker
sniff

snoop
snow
snug

sm

smack
small
smart

smash
smear
smell

smile
smoke
smooth

sph

sphere

spinx

sp

space
spaghetti
spanking
spare
spark
speak
spoon

spear
special
speck
spice
spider
spin
spit

sport
spoil
spoke
spot
wasp
crisp
grasp

spl

splash splice split
splint

spr

sprain spread spruce
spray spring sprout
sprinkle

squ

squad squat squeeze
square squabble squirm
squash squeal squirrel
squirt

st

stage state toast
stain station wrist
steak stay list
stamp steep test
stand step rest
stem stop waste
stew stir last
star cost

str

straight strike street
straw strip strict
stream stroke string
stretch stranger stripe
strat strong

sw

swallow swell swear
sway swing sweep
sweet swamp swim
switch

Hidden Pictures

sailboat ⛵ soap 🧼
salt 🧂 softball ⚾
saw 🪚 soup 🥫
seahorse 🌱 sun ☀
six 6 sundae 🍨

Name_____ Date_____

Supercalifragilisticexpialidocious

Directions: One of the longest words in the English language is *supercalifragilisticexpialidocious*, 34 letters. See how many words you can make that begin with *s*. Remember to think of words that start with *sa, se, si, so, su, sl,* and *sp*. List them in the blanks below.

supercalifragilisticexpialidocious

1. _____   6. _____

2. _____   7. _____

3. _____   8. _____

4. _____   9. _____

5. _____   10. _____

sh
as in *shark*

Introducing /sh/

1. Ask the children whether they know how to tell someone softly to be quiet. The children should say /sh/. If not, say it to them. When you say it, write *sh* on the board. Now tell the children that you know a word with *sh* at the end that means "be quiet." Ask whether they can think of what it is. If they cannot think of the word *hush,* tell them. As you say the word, emphasize the /sh/ at the end.

2. Tell the children you know many words that begin or end with the /sh/ sound. Write some of these words on the board: *shade, shake, shame, shape, share, sharp, shave, she, sheep, shirt, shot, short, shoot, shoe, shack, should, shy, cash, flash, rash, splash, trash, dish, fish, wish, brush,* and *rush.* Say these words, emphasizing the /sh/ sound.

3. Now have the children look at the list of hidden objects that begin with sh. Have them emphasize /sh/ as they say the words. They can find the objects in the picture and tell you what they have found.

203

Reinforcing /sh/

Tell the children you have a story about a man called Mr. Shing Shang. He is a happy fellow, but he hates to get up in the morning. Ask them whether they like to, and then you might want to talk about bad mornings and good mornings. Hand out the activity page, and then have the children complete the story by making this either a good or a bad morning for Mr. Shing Shang. As they read the story about Mr. Shing Shang, they should try to find all the /sh/ sounds in the story. Direct them to circle the /sh/ at the beginning or at the end of the words.

Working with Words for /sh/

You may want to review the difference between a consonant blend and a consonant digraph. A consonant blend is a combination of two or three speech sounds blended together to make one sound that consists of a little bit of each sound; a consonant digraph is a combination of two consonants that represents a *new* speech sound. Demonstrate the difference by having the children say some of the blends found in the lesson plan for /s/. Use the following words to demonstrate the /sh/ sound:

sh

she	shot	shape
should	shag	shake
show	shore	shall
shade	shine	ship
shout	shoes	shut
short	shed	shop
		shock

-sh

trash	rush	wash
fish	crush	brush
		fresh

Hidden Pictures

shark
shawl
shelf
shell
shovel

sherbet
ship
shirt
shoe

BAKE SHOP

Name_____ Date_____

Mr. Shing Shang

Directions: Read the story about Mr. Shing Shang, a man who hated to get up in the morning. After you read the story, write an ending to it on the back of this page. You can make Mr. Shing Shang have a bad morning or a good morning. When you have finished writing the story, go back through the entire story and circle the /sh/ sounds, as in Mr. Shing Shang's name.

Mr. Shing Shang hated to get up in the morning. First he had to shave with a sharp razor. Then he took a shower. He usually used shampoo to wash his hair. Then he had to shine his shoes. Finally, he could put on his shirt and pants.

Mr. Shing Shang then looked on the shelf for his favorite cereal. He always shut the cupboard door quietly so he did not wake up the children. He then began to shake some cereal into his bowl.

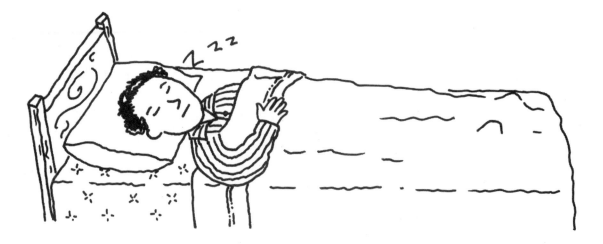

t
as in *turtle*

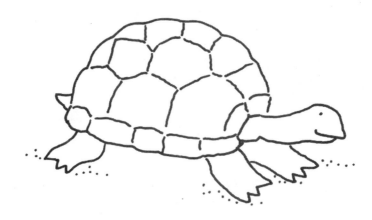

Introducing /t/

1. You might want to begin teaching the sound of *t* by asking the children to tell you what noise they make when they tickle another person. Most of the children will say, /t/, /t/, /t/, /t/. If they do not say this sound, say it for them.

2. Provide each child with two index cards. One card should say *yes*, the other card should say *no*. As you recite the following words, the children should hold up the *yes* card when the word begins with /t/. If the word does not begin with /t/, they should hold up the *no* card. Use

the words *table, took, take, bake, top, tea, Dan, Tom, Terry, toss, paper, turkey, to, tell, time, clock,* and *telephone.* Now ask the children to think of some words that begin with /t/ and to be the "teacher" as the others hold up their *yes* or *no* cards.

3. Give the children the list of the hidden objects. Have them notice the letter *t* and emphasize the /t/ as they say the name of each object. As the children find the objects in the picture, again emphasize the /t/ sound.

Reinforcing /t/

Tell the children that Tom and Pat are going to town to look for toys. Tom gets to keep all of the toys that begin with /t/ (*teddy bear, turtle, teacups,* and *top*). Pat gets all of those that end with /t/ (*boat, jet, kite, art kit*). They share those toys that begin *and* end with /t/ (*tent, target,* and *tennis*

racquet). Hand out the activity page. Direct the children to write each toy under the name of the child who owns it. After the children have completed the activity, have them read the names of the toys that they found in the picture. Direct them to listen to the /t/.

Working with Words for /t/

1. The /t/ is found at the beginning of many sound patterns. Use these words to teach /t/:

tip	tag	tug	top	tail
tack	tin	tan	tank	tow
tell	tan	test	tap	Ted
tore	tail	take	tight	tab
tuck	Tim	till	tip	tick

2. The sound of *t* is heard in the final position of many sound patterns and words. Use the following words to help children learn the sound patterns with /t/, and at the same time review appropriate vowel principles.

at

at	flat	rat
bat	hat	sat
cat	mat	that
fat	pat	

eat

eat	heat	pleat
beat	meat	treat
cheat	neat	wheat

ate

ate	hate	rate
date	late	skate
gate	plate	state

irt

dirt	flirt	shirt
	squirt	skirt

et

bet   let   set
get   met   vet
jet   pet   wet
                 yet

it

bit   knit   sit
fit   mitt   skit
it   pit   spit
kit   quit

ight

bright height night
fight   light   knight
flight might right
                sight

est

best   pest   test
nest   rest   vest
              chest

ite

bite kite white
     spite write

oat

boat coat float

ot

blot got   not
cot   hot   pot
dot knot rot
     lot   shot
          spot

ut

but cut putt
    hut rut
    nut shut

3. The letter *t* is combined with *r* or *w* to from the consonant blends *tr* and *tw*. You can use the following words to help children learn to say only one sound when they see these letter combinations.

tw

tweed	twin	twirl
tweezers	twice	twine
twelve	twist	twilight
twenty	twiddle	twinkle

tr

trace	tribe	try
train	trunk	tree
triangle	tractor	tray
trouble	travel	trail
track	trick	traffic
trap	trust	treat

4. The letter *t* follows the letters *f, l, n,* or *s* to form consonant blends commonly found at the end of words. Some words to use in the "Working with Words" activity follow. Other words can be found in the lesson plans for *f, l, n,* and *s*.

lt

halt	felt	built
belt	melt	tilt
	knelt	

ft

left	raft	drift
soft	theft	lift
		swift

st

cost	last	fist
pest	chest	dust
fast		

nt

went	ant	don't
dent	sent	front
	mint	

Hidden Pictures

tack

teacup

tent

tie

toast

toe

tomato

turtle

Name_____ Date_____

Toys for Tots

Directions: Tom and Pat went to town to look for toys. Tom gets to keep the toys that begin with /t/. Pat gets those that end with /t/. They share the toys that begin *and* end with /t/. Write the toys under their names.

 TOM

PAT

/th/ and /th/, as in
feather and *thumb*

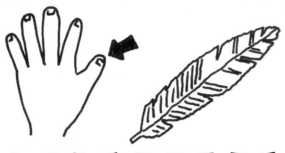

Introducing /*th*/ and /th/

1. Begin this lesson by writing *th* on the board. Tell the children the letters *t* and *h* combine to make two new sounds. Sometimes the sound is like /th/, as in *thank, thick, think,* and *thief* (voiceless). Other times when *t* and *h* are together, they sound like /th/, as in *than, that, then, the, this,* and *there* (voiced).

2. Tell the children you are going to say some words that have one of the *th* sounds at the beginning. If you are saying /th/, as in *think* (voiceless), the children should point their fingers to their heads. If you are say-ing /th/, as in *there* (voiced), they should point their fingers below their Adam's apples.

3. Explain to the children that they may feel the voiced-*th* sound by putting their fingers right below their Adam's apples. Tell them their vocal chords are located there and that when they say /th/, as in *there,* they may feel the vocal chords move.

4. When they say the voiceless-*th* sound, as in *thick, thought,* or *think,* they will not feel the vibrations; how-ever, the children can feel an increase in the air coming out of their mouths. Have the children say *thank*, *thumb*, and *thing*. As they say these words, they will feel air coming through their lips.

5. Some children have a difficult time hearing the difference between the two sounds of *th*. Do not spend hours trying to help the children discriminate these sounds; it is more important for them to realize that when *t* and *h* are combined, they produce *one* speech sound. Trying one of these sounds along with using context clues should enable the children to pronounce an unfamiliar word.

For example, if a child is reading the sentence "Tom ordered a *thick* milk shake," and the word *thick* appears unfamiliar, the child will realize that *t* and *h* produce one sound, try the sound that they know, and then will know whether they are right or wrong by the context.

6. All of the hidden objects have the voiceless-*th* sound. You may want to have the children feel the air coming out of their lips when they say this sound. As the children find the objects, have them emphasize the /*th*/ sound.

Reinforcing /*th*/ and /th/

This reinforcement activity is designed to help children hear the difference between the two sounds of *th*. As you look at "Get That Thief!", you will notice the words in the left half of the circle contain the voiceless-*th* sound; the words in the right half of the circle have the voiced-*th* sound. This activity will give the children many opportunities to read both sounds of *th*. To begin the game, one child or team is designat-ed as Thinny and the other as Thatty. The player or teams then throw a die. Thinny moves to the left to catch the thief. Thatty move to the right and tries to get the thief first. The first team or player to throw exactly the right number to land on the thief is the winner. Have the children take turns being Thinny and Thatty so they have an opportunity to read words containing both sounds of *th*.

Working with Words for /th/ and /th/

1. Words you can use during "Working with Words" to help children learn the voiceless-*th* sound include:

Initial Position		Final Position
thank	thumb	teeth
think	thirst	math
thick	thong	cloth
thing	thought	moth
thief	thimble	bath
thin	third	path
		truth

2. Words for teaching the voiced-*th* sound are as follows:

Initial Position	Middle or Final Position	
that	mother	father
then	brother	feather
thus	weather	gather
the	bother	together
than	rather	other
them	either	neither
there	breathe	teethe
this		
though		

Hidden Pictures

thermometer
thief
thimble
thirty
thong
thorn
thumb
thumbtack

Name_____ Date_____

Get That Thief!

Directions: That thief has done it again! He has gotten away with the goods. See if you can catch him. Two people can play. One player is called Thinny. The other player is called Thatty. Thinny goes to the left and tries to catch the thief. Thatty goes to the right and tries to catch the thief. Decide who goes first. Throw a die to see how many spaces you can move. The first one to throw the exact number of spaces to land on the thief is the winner. Go get 'em!

as in *truck*

 **Introducing /ŭ/**

1. Ask the children if they have ever heard someone who had a hard time thinking of what to say and said /ŭ/. Tell them this person was actually saying the short u sound. Write these words on the board with the missing letter. Have the children add u to the letters to make words with the /ŭ/ sound.

h——m	r——sh	d——ck
t——b	——s	c——t
dr——m	g——m	f——n

Read all the words with the children and emphasize the short u sound.

2. Now direct the children's attention to the picture of the hidden objects. Have them trace the letter u as they say the words, emphasizing the short u sound. As they find the objects in the picture, review the short u sound.

Reinforcing /ŭ/

1. Ask the children what kinds of cereals they like and discuss why they buy certain cereals. Tell them the activity they have today involves the back of a cereal box. The name of the cereal is "Munch and Crunch." Ask the children what vowel sound they hear in *munch* and *crunch* and how this cereal would taste.

2. Tell them that there is a game on the cereal box. Hand out the activity sheet. The children are to find as many words as they can that have the same vowel sound as in *munch* and *crunch* (short *u*). Tell the children they can go up, down, across, or diagonally, as long as the letters are next to each other. After finding the words, children should check to see what free gifts they've won. The

children should be able to find these short *u* words:

sum	cub	us
such	bus	duck
dust	cud	bud
dumb	hum	stuck
suds	rub	rum
drum	crumb	sub
tub	hub	much
bum	thumb	but
thus	thud	cut

3. List the words as the children find them, and read them again, emphasizing the short *u* sound. Point out that all of the words end in a consonant; this is a clue that the *u* has the /ŭ/ sound.

Working with Words for /ŭ/

Common phonograms you can use in teaching /ŭ/ include:

uck

struck	stuck	tuck
suck	truck	Chuck
duck	buck	cluck
	luck	pluck

ub

grub	stub	sub
scrub	club	tub
snub	cub	shrub
	rub	

ŭ

ug
bug
dug
rug
mug

plug
slug
snug
tug

jug
chug
drug
shrug

um
bum
drum
dumb
numb

hum
gum
rum
slum
mum

sum
chum
plum
strum
swum

umb
dumb

numb
crumb

plumb
thumb

ump
bump
dump
grump

pump
hump
lump

jump
stump
thump

un
bun
fun

run
spun

sun

unch
bunch
crunch

hunch
munch

punch
scrunch
lunch

ung

hung
lung
rung
stung
sung
strung
swung
young

unt

bunt
hunt
punt
stunt
runt
blunt
grunt

ush

brush
crush
flush
hush
rush
lush
blush
plush
slush

ut

but
cut
hut
shut
nut
gut
rut
strut

unk

bunk
drunk
flunk
skunk
sunk
dunk
funk
junk
chunk
plunk
shrunk
stunk
trunk

ust

dust
just
rust
must
trust

Hidden Pictures

brush
cup
duck
gum
gun
truck
tub
umbrella

Name_____ Date_____

Munch and Crunch

Directions: This cereal box has lots of words that have the short *u* sound, as in *munch* and *crunch*. See how many short *u* words you can find. In order to find words, you can go up, down, across, or diagonally, but the letters must be next to each other. The prize that you get inside the box depends on the number of words you find. After you have found the words, look for your prize.

If you find 1–5 words, you get a piece of gum.
If you find 6–10 words, the prize is a cup.
If you find 11–15 words, you get a drum.
If you find 16–20 words, you get a duck.
If you find 21–25 words, you have won a bunny.

Circle Your Prize!

1. _____
2. _____
3. _____
4. _____
5. _____
6. _____
7. _____
8. _____
9. _____
10. _____
11. _____
12. _____
13. _____

14. _____
15. _____
16. _____
17. _____
18. _____
19. _____
20. _____
21. _____
22. _____
23. _____
24. _____
25. _____

ū

as in *unicycle*

Introducing /ū/

1. Say to the children, "You are going to learn a new vowel sound that sounds like the word *you*." Ask the children to guess what sound it is. Write these words on the board: *juice, use, blue, tube,* and *cute.* Pronounce them for the children. Next have the children say the words with you and emphasize the long *u* sound.

2. Tell them that today the words that are hidden all have the long *u* sound, even though they do not have the letter *u* in them. Say the words so the children can hear /ū/. Explain to the children that sometimes letter combinations such as *ew* can make the /ū/ sound. Have the children find the hidden objects in the picture and emphasize the /ū/ sound.

Reinforcing /ū/

Ask the children whether they have ever tried to ride a unicycle. Tell them it is hard to do but they can do it today if they can read the words that have the long u sound, as in *unicycle*. Hand out the activity page. Direct the children to throw a die to find out how many spaces they can move. If they move to a word and can read it, they can stay there. If not, they must go back, because they have fallen off the unicycle. The first one to land on the finish line by an exact throw is the winner. Read the words with the children so they again have a chance to hear the long u sound. You may want to point out the different spellings of the long u sound, such as the *ew* spelling in *blew*, *chew*, *drew*, *few*, *brew*, *threw*, *new*, and *jewel*.

Working with Words for /ū/

1. Sometimes *u* is long because it is the vowel in a syllable or word ending with a silent *e*. Use these phonograms to review the silent *e* principle:

ube
cube   lube   tube

uce
spruce   truce

ude
dude   nude   crude
         rude   prude

uke
duke   nuke   fluke

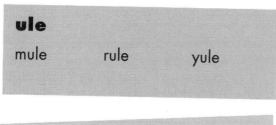

ule

mule   rule   yule

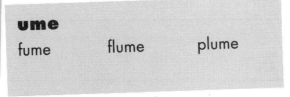

ume

fume   flume   plume

une

June   tune   prune

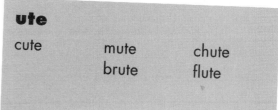

ute

cute   mute   chute
         brute   flute

2. In some dictionaries and reading series the *ew* combination is pronounced as long *u*. Some dictionaries and reading series, however, say that the *ew* combination represents the long *oo* sound, as in *tool*. You should teach the children the sound–symbol relationship that appears in your reading series. Use these words during "Working with Words" to teach the *ew* sound pattern:

ew

dew	blew	flew
few	brew	grew
knew	crew	screw
new	chew	stew
pew	drew	threw

Hidden Pictures

canoe
cube
flute
glue
perfume
screw
ukulele
unicycle

Unicycle Race

Directions: How good are you at riding a unicycle? Two players can have a race. Put a token on Start for each player. Throw a die to see how many spaces you can move. Move to that space if you are able to read the word. If not, you have fallen and you must go back to Start. The first one to reach the finish line by an exact throw is the winner.

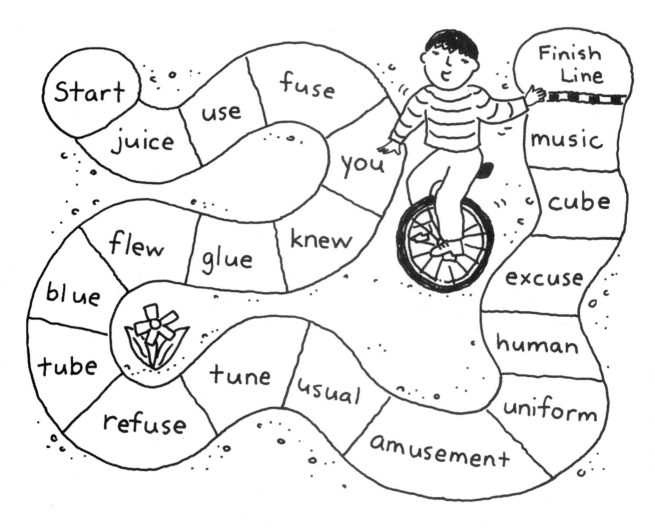

V
as in *vase*

Introducing /v/

1. Tell children the sound they are going to learn is /v/, as in *very*. Then write the following words on the board and read each one as you write it: *vote, voice, vanilla, velvet, valentine,* and *visit*. Ask the children what sound all of these words have at the beginning. As they say /v/, have them feel their teeth rest on their lower lips.

2. Show them the list of objects that begin with /v/. Have the children trace the *vs* as they say the words. Now direct them to find the objects in the picture and to use the words in sentences.

Reinforcing /v/

Divide students into cooperative groups of two or three. Distribute a copy of "Volcano," a spinner, and tokens to each group. Read the words aloud on the game board with the class. Instruct students to take turns spinning the spinner and moving the number of spaces. If the students can read the /v/ word, they stay on the spot; if not, they remain on their previous spot. The first student to reach the end is the winner.

Working with Words for /v/

1. Use these words to teach the sound of /v/ in the initial position:

van   vest   vine   vail   vain   vow

2. The sound of *v* is found in the final position of many words. You can use the following words during "Working with Words" to help the children hear the /v/ in the final position.

brave	cave	grave	wave
they've	pave	eve	leave
sleeve	weave	give	five
live	hive	I've	drive
glove	love	stove	we've

Hidden Pictures

vacuum
valentine
van
vase
vessel
vest

violet
violin
vitamins
volcano
volleyball

Name_____ Date_____

Volcano

Directions: Spin the spinner and move that number of spaces. If you can read the word on that space, stay there. If not, return to your previous spot. The first one to the end is the winner.

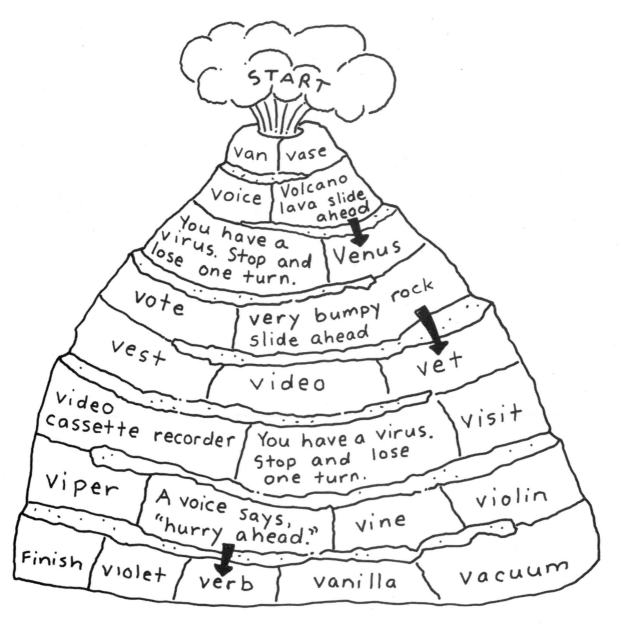

as in *wagon*

Introducing /w/

1. Duplicate the following story. Tell the children that today they are going to work on /w/, as in *wagon* and *wafer*. Direct the children's attention to the story. Read the story with them to find all the words that begin with /w/. Circle these words as you read the story.

Wally went for a walk with his wagon. He saw a woman walking to work. Soon Wally was warm. He waded in a puddle. Wally splashed water up to his waist. It was fun, but he knew his mom would be mad.

His pants had to be washed. Wally wiped off his pants and walked home.

His mother said, "How did you get all wet?" Wally told her and began to weep. His mother said, "I know you were warm, but you should wait to put on your swimming suit. You're not a worm!" She winked and said, "Here is a wafer. Let's forget this."

Wally smiled and said, "I won't do that again. Next time I'll come home for a wafer!"

2. After the children have enjoyed the story, go back and read all of the circled words so the children can hear the /w/ and see the symbol that represents it.

3. Now show the children the list of the hidden objects. As they say each object, emphasize the /w/ sound.

Reinforcing /w/

Tell the children today they are going to play a game called "Walk and Wait." Ask the children where they have seen these words. Perhaps they are written on the traffic signals near the school. Hand out the activity sheet. Two players or two teams can play this game. Direct the children to take turns throwing a die. They move ahead the number of spaces shown on the die. If they are able to read the word, they stay on the space. If not, they move back until they can read a word. The first team or player to reach the word *winner* by an exact throw wins. You may want to go over the words with the children before they use this activity independently. As you do so, emphasize the /w/.

Working with Words for /w/

1. Words using the most common phonograms you can use in teaching /w/ in the initial position are:

way   will   wag   well   wing   west

weed   wink   wow   wore   wine

wed   wake   wick   wall   win

2. The children will soon learn that *w* can also act like a vowel, as in *law*, *cow*, and *few*. Special attention is paid to these sounds in the lesson plans for the vowel sounds. At this point, simply help the children realize that when *w* is in the final position, it acts like a vowel and does not sound like /w/.

Hidden Pictures

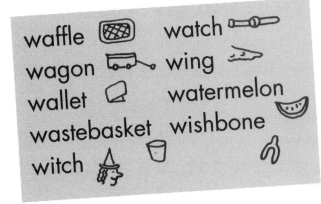

waffle
wagon
wallet
wastebasket
witch

watch
wing
watermelon
wishbone

Name_____ Date_____

Walk and Wait

Directions: Two players or teams can play this game. Throw a die to see how many spaces you can move ahead. If you can read the word, you get to stay on the space where you have landed. If not, you move back to the first word you can read. Sometimes you will be walking; other times you will be waiting. The first team or player to reach the word *winner* by an exact throw wins!

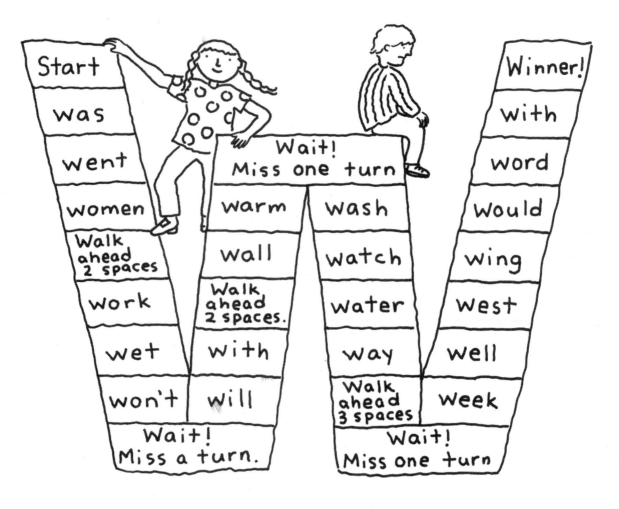

wh

as in *wheel*

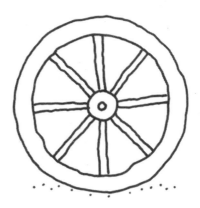

Introducing /wh/

1. Tell the children you are going to see whether they can guess what you are pantomiming. All the words that you are going to pantomime begin with /wh/, as in *which*. First, pretend that you are rubbing whiskers on your face. Then pretend that you are whistling. Now act as though you are whispering something. Finally, pretend that you are whipping something by hitting your hand against your leg. Write the words on the board: *whiskers, whistle, whisper,* and *whip*.

2. Have the children say the words and ask them to think of others that begin with the same sound. They may suggest *why, wheat, wheel, what, whale, whammy, whether, where,* or *when*.

3. Tell the children that all of today's hidden objects begin with /wh/. Have them say the names of the objects and notice the *wh* at the beginning. Tell them that *w* and *h* make one sound when they are together. Isolate the sound and have the children trace the *wh* as they say each word. Now give them the picture, and as they tell you what they have found, emphasize the /wh/.

Reinforcing /wh/

Students reinforce /wh/ by playing the game "Whoa" in teams of two to four players. Give each group a game board, tokens, and spinner or dice. Students take turns rolling the dice to see how many spaces they move. If the student can read the /wh/ word, they stay on the space. The first team to the end wins!

Working with Words for /wh/

1. Some dictionaries do not consider /wh/ a distinctive speech sound in English. If your reading series does not, simply teach it as a consonant cluster—two consonants that represent one sound. Words you can use in teaching /wh/ are:

what	wheat
whack	white
which	whirl
while	whiz
whisper	wheels
when	where

Hidden Pictures

whale
wheat
wheel
wheelbarrow

whip
whisk broom
whiskers
whistle

Name_____ Date_____

Whoa!

Directions: Two to four players play Whoa! Each player needs a token to put on Start. Throw the dice to see how many spaces you can move. If you can read the word, you stay on the space. The first one to the end wins the game.

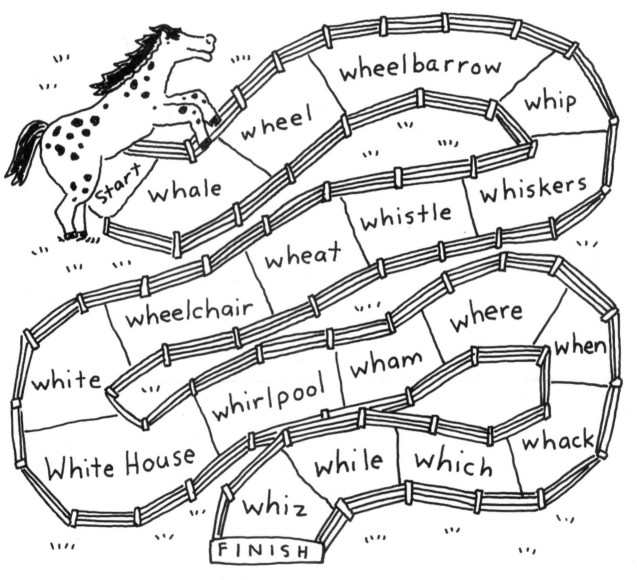

= /eks/ as in *X ray*

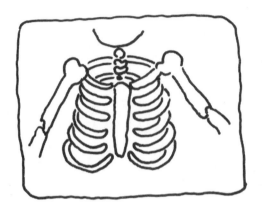

Introducing the /eks/ Sound of *x*

1. Begin this lesson by playing a game of "Xs and Os" with the children. Divide the group members into two teams; designate one X and one O. After you have played the game, ask the children what sound of *o* they are saying when they say, "o." They should say /ō/. Then ask them what sound they are saying when they say, "x." They should be able to hear the /eks/. If not, tell them that when they say the name of *x*, they are really saying /eks/. Tell them the letter *x* does not have its own sound, but rather sounds like /ks/ at the end of many words.

2. Write these words on the board: *box, fix, six, tax, mix,* and *wax*. Have the children say the words and listen to the last sound they are saying. They should be able to hear the /ks/ blend.

3. Now direct the children's attention to the list of hidden objects. As the children find the objects in the picture, have them emphasize the /ks/ sound. Conclude the lesson by asking the children what sound *x* represents in the final position of words or syllables.

Reinforcing the /eks/ Sound of *x*

Divide the class into groups of two. Distribute the game board, spinner, and tokens. Tell the class they are trying to reach Mexico or Texas for vacation. Students take turns spinning the spinner and reading the word with an *x*. If they pronounce the word correctly, the student remains on the spot. The first person to Mexico or Texas is the winner.

Working with Words for the /eks/ Sound of *x*

The *x* can also sound like /z/, as in *xylophone*. Since there are not many words in which the *x* represents /z/, it is wise to teach these words as sight words. You can review the fact that *x* can have the /z/ sound when you teach the /gz/ sound of *x*.

Hidden Pictures

ax
exit
fox
mixer
six
taxi

Name_____ Date_____

Mexico or Texas

Directions: You are trying to make it to Mexico or Texas for vacation. Take turns spinning the spinner. If you can read the word, you stay on the spot; if not, remain where you were. The first person to make it to Mexico or Texas is the winner.

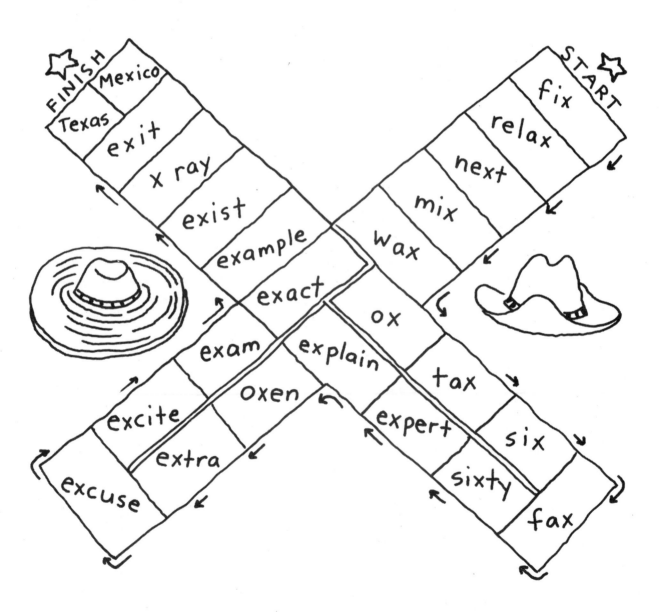

y

as in *yo-yo*

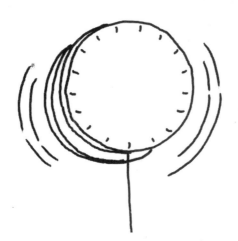

Introducing /y/

1. Begin the lesson by telling the children you have a "two-way" letter in your pocket. Ask them what *two-way* means. Perhaps they associate this concept with a two-way street. If the children are not sure of your letter, give them these clues:

It begins like one of the colors. (yellow)

It is what you say when you eat something that you like. ("Yummy")

When you shake your head up and down, you are saying _____ . (yes)

If someone is very angry, he might begin to _____ loudly. (yell)

I have mine and you have _____ . (yours)

Ask the children how all of these words begin. After they point out the /y/ sound, show them your two-way letter.

2. Ask them why you call it a *two-way letter.* If they do not know, write these common words on the board: *they, very, day, boy, why,* and *many.* Tell the children to listen as you read these words to see whether they hear the /y/ sound. Of course, the children will hear sounds other than /y/. Now see whether they can tell you why you call it a *two-way letter*. If the children are not sure, tell them the letter *y* can either be a consonant or a vowel. Today you are going to work on the consonant sound of *y*. Tell the children that when *y* is a consonant they will always find it at the beginning of a word or syllable.

3. Now give the children the list of hidden objects. Have them trace the *y* as they say each word. Direct them to find the objects in the picture and review the sound as they find the hidden objects.

Reinforcing /y/

Tell the children there is a favorite toy that begins with /y/. See whether they can think of the word *yo-yo*. Tell them you want to find out whether they can do "Around the World" with a yo-yo. Either explain or demonstrate how this is done. You begin with the yo-yo down by your knees and bring it up and all the way around so it comes back to your knees. This trick is called "Around the World" because you are making a circle, the shape of the world.

In order for them to go "around the world," they will have to spin a spinner to see how many turns they get. They should then move the indicated number of spaces and read what their special message is. The winner is the person who first spins the *exact* number of spaces needed to reach "You made it!" Review the /y/ sound by having the children read the words that begin with /y/.

Working with Words for /y/

1. *Y* serves as a vowel most of the time; rarely is it a consonant. The vowel sound of *y* is usually long *e* (as in *happy*), long *i* (as in *type*), or short *i* (as in *hymn* or *myth*). *Y* is combined with *o* to form the diphthong as in *toy*; it also forms the vowel digraphs *ay* (as in *day*) and *ey* (as in *key*). More information concerning these special sounds of *y* is presented in the lesson plans on long *a*, long *e*, long *i*, and short *i*.

2. The children will learn that *y* functions as a vowel when a word has no other vowel (*by*); *y* is at the end of a word (*happy*); and *y* follows another vowel (*day*, *key*, *joy*). Words to use in the "Working with Words" activity are:

y = /ē/	**y = /ī/**		**y = /ĭ/**
candy	cry	ply	gym
berry	try	shy	gyp
nasty	my	sky	cyst
party	by	sly	system
scary	fly	spy	bicycle
weary	sky	spry	antonym
carry	spry	thy	homonym
tasty	rely	try	synonym
	supply	dry	
	why	fry	
	why		

Hidden Pictures

yacht
yardstick
yarn
yellow jacket
yield
yogurt
yoke
yo-yo

Name_____ Date_____

Around the World

Directions: See which team can go around the world first with this yo-yo. In order to do so, spin a spinner to see how many spaces you can move. Then read what it says on the spaces so you know whether you should stay there, move ahead, or move back. The first one to spin the exact number of spaces needed to land on "You made it!" is the winner.

Z
as in *zebra*

 ## Introducing /z/

1. Ask the children whether they have ever been to the zoo. If so, what kind of animals did they see? Ask them whether they saw an animal whose name begins with the same sound as *zoo*. They will probably mention the *zebra*, but if they do not, you can tell them. Write the words *zoo* and *zebra* on the board and give the children dictionaries to find other words that begin with /z/, such as *zero, zap, zipper, zoom, zone,* and *zenith.*

2. Now write the words *fizz, quiz,* and *whiz* on the board. Ask the children to notice the letter *z* and the /z/ sound at the end of these words. Tell them the *z* can be found either at the beginning or at the end of a word or syllable.

3. Now direct the children's attention to the list of hidden objects. Say the name of each object and again have them notice the /z/ sound. You can point out that the word *xylophone* begins with *x* but has the sound of *z*. Tell the children that *x* can also make the /z/ sound, since it does not have a sound of its own. Now have the children find the objects in the picture. As they find them, again review the /z/ sound.

Reinforcing /z/

Tell the children that some zebras with zero stripes are in a zigzag cage in the zoo. Hand out the activity page, and ask students to put stripes on the zebras by finding words that begin with /z/. They should begin at Start and move as the hands of a clock do. Tell them that if a word begins with /z/,

they should write it on the zebra at the top. If the word ends with /z/, they should make the stripe on the zebra at the bottom. The children will find and write the words *zap, zero, zoo, zone, zoom,* and *zip* on the *zebra* at the top. The zebra on the bottom will have stripes with the words *fizz, quiz,* and *jazz.*

Working with Words for /z/

1. Review the fact that the letter *s* can represent /z/ at the end of many words. You can refer to the lesson plan for the sound of *s* to find the sample words.

2. Additional words for teaching /z/ are:

zap	zinc	zone
zero	zip code	zonked
zest	zipper	zoom
zigzag	zodiac	zoology

Hidden Pictures

xylophone zigzag
zebra zinnia
zero zipper

Name_____ Date_____

Zebras with Zero Stripes in a Zigzag Cage

Directions: The two zebras in the zigzag cage look funny because they do not have any stripes. You can give them stripes by finding words that begin or end with /z/. Begin where it says Start, and, if you find a word that begins with /z/, write it on the zebra at the top. If the word ends with /z/, write it on the zebra at the bottom. You will have to make stripes in which to write your words. The first one is done for you. Do the others and then color the zebras.

as in *banana*

Introducing the Schwa Sound

1. Begin this lesson by reminding the children that every syllable must have a vowel sound. Explain that since the vowel sound has to appear in every syllable, sometimes it is difficult to hear the vowel sound—especially in the unaccented syllables (the syllables you hardly hear). Usually the vowel sound in an unaccented syllable is difficult to isolate—yet it is there, because all syllables must have a vowel sound. Tell the children the vowel sound they hear in the unaccented syllables is called the *schwa sound*. The schwa sound sounds almost like short *u*, but you do not hear or say it as loudly.

2. Tell the children that all five vowel letters can represent the schwa sound. For example, in the word *macaroni*, the second *a* represents the schwa sound. The *e* represents the schwa sound in *camel*, the *i* in *helicopter*, the *o* in *lemon*, and the second *u* in *ukulele*. Write these five words on the board and have the children say them. As they say them, they should be listening for the schwa sound, which is difficult to hear because it is in the unaccented syllable. Do not have the children overstress the schwa sound, or the word will not sound right.

3. Tell the children that all of the hidden objects have the schwa sound. Show them the list of the objects and have them point out the schwa sound in each word: banana, candle, lemon, pencil, seven, shovel, tuba, and umbrella. Now they can find the hidden objects in the picture.

Reinforcing the Schwa Sound

Tell the children the SWAT team is looking for the schwa sound. There is one schwa sound hiding in each corner of this star-shaped building on the activity sheet. When the children find the word with the schwa sound, they should write it in the center of the building, which is serving as a "temporary jail." When the children have finished this activity, have them read the words and point out the schwa sound. They can then make a special SWAT team badge to wear.

Working with Words for the Schwa Sound

1. Tell the children words that end with *le* usually have the schwa sound. This is especially true of the words that have the *ble*, *dle*, *fle*, *gle*, *kle*, *ple*, *tle*, and *zle* endings. The syllable is generally pronounced /el/, since the last syllable in the words that end with *le* is generally not accented. This might be a good time to teach the children that when they come to a word that ends in *le*, the consonant preceding the *le* usually goes with it to form the final syllable. This rule for dividing words into syllables will give children some clue as to the sound of the last syllable. You can point out that the *e* is silent and that the vowel sound is the schwa, as in /el/. Sample words are:

dle

candle   noodles   middle

ble

bubbles   marble   table

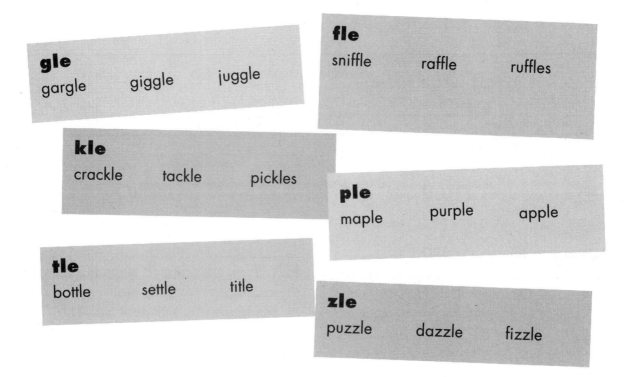

gle
gargle   giggle   juggle

fle
sniffle   raffle   ruffles

kle
crackle   tackle   pickles

ple
maple   purple   apple

tle
bottle   settle   title

zle
puzzle   dazzle   fizzle

2. If the children need more practice in identifying the schwa sound, it is possible to open the dictionary to any page and find the schwa sound in the respelling of at least one word on that page. Words that you can use during "Working with Words" for this sound are as follows:

machine	compass	button	person
ago	again	above	around
second	helicopter	company	president
several	busily	beautiful	reason
among	happen	idea	parade

Hidden Pictures

banana
candle
lemon
pencil
seven
shovel
tuba
umbrella

Name_____ Date_____

The SWAT Team

Directions: The SWAT team is looking for schwa sounds. There is one schwa sound in a word in each corner of the star-shaped building. Read each word and find the one with the schwa sound. When you find it, write it in the center of the star, which is going to serve as a temporary jail. After you have completed the activity, turn the paper over, trace the star, and make a special SWAT team badge to wear.

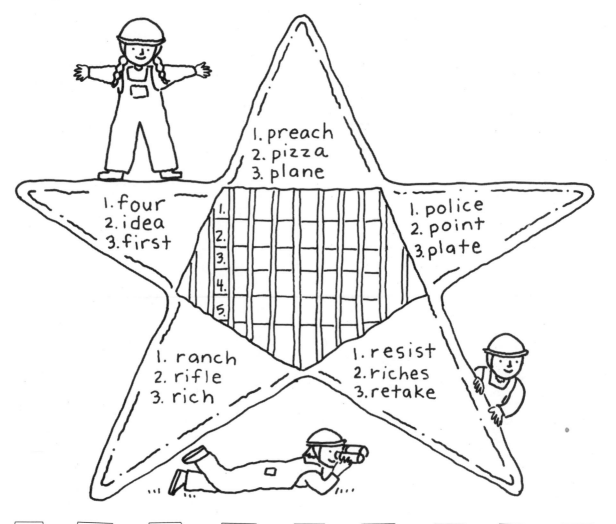

1. preach
2. pizza
3. plane

1. four
2. idea
3. first

1. police
2. point
3. plate

1.
2.
3.
4.
5.

1. ranch
2. rifle
3. rich

1. resist
2. riches
3. retake

Appendix A Blank Script

The following blank "Working with Words" script can also be used by support personnel who work with your students to provide individual or small-group instruction. The blank script can also be used as a guide for personnel such as volunteers who have not been trained to use the "Working with Words" activities. Duplicate the script for the volunteer, paraprofessional, etc., and complete the blank sections that require the specific information for your lesson. Emphasize to the support personnel leading this lesson that they must use the word in a sentence as students are manipulating the letters on their desks.

Blank Script

Begin instruction by telling students to place their consonant(s) and vowels on top of their desks in alphabetical order. Write the consonant(s) and phonograms on the chalkboard or place the large letters in the pocket chart.

T: I would like you to put the consonant(s) _____ and the vowels _____ on your desk in alphabetical order as I write these on the chalkboard.

Say aloud the sound of the consonant(s) _____ and vowels _____ as you point to them on the chalkboard or pocket chart.

T: Let's say the sound the letter(s) _____ makes, /__/. You will hear /___/ in all of the words we make today. Let's also say the letters and sound in each one of the word families or phonograms:

_____. Great job everyone! Let's start making some words.

Instruct students to place the letter(s) _____ in front of them on their desks. Using one phonogram at a time, have students move the letters of the phonogram from the top of their desks next to the consonant(s) _____. Say the word aloud as well as in a sentence. After students have time to make the word, look around the classroom and have a student with the correct answer say and spell the word aloud. Ask this child to spell the word using the large letters in the pocket chart.

T: Place the letter(s) _____ in front of you on your desk. I would like you to find the letters of the word family or phonogram _____ (point to them) and move them next to the consonant(s) _____ to make the word _____ (insert a sentence here using the target word). Great, I see (insert child's name) has this one correct. Please spell _____ for us. Does everyone hear the /_____/ sound? Let's

say _____ together. Come spell _____ using the pocket chart.

T: Put the word family or phonogram _____ back and get the letters of the phonogram _____ (point to them). **Place them next to the letter(s) _____ to make the word _____** (insert a sentence here using the target word). **Great, I see** (insert child's name) **has this one correct. Please spell -_____ for us. Does everyone hear the /____/ sound? Let's say _____ together. Come spell _____ using the pocket chart.**

T: Put the word family or phonogram _____ back and find the letters of the phonogram _____ (point to them). **Place them next to the letter(s) _____ to make the word _____** (insert a sentence here using the target word). **Great, I see** (insert child's name) **has this one correct. Please spell _____ for us. Does everyone hear the /____/ sound? Let's say _____ together. Come spell _____ using the pocket chart.**

T: Put the word family or phonogram _____ back and find the letters of the phonogram _____ (point to them). **Place them next to the letter(s) _____ to make the word _____** (insert a sentence here using the target word). **Great, I see** (insert child's name) **has this one correct. Please spell _____ for us. Does everyone hear the /____/ sound? Let's say _____ together. Come spell _____ using the pocket chart.**

T: Put the word family or phonogram _____ back and get the phonogram _____ (point to them). **Place**

them next to the letter(s) to make the word _____ (insert a sentence here using the target word). **Great, I see** (insert child's name) **has this one correct. Please spell _____ for us. Does everyone hear the /____/ sound? Let's say _____ together. Come spell _____ using the pocket chart.**

T: Put the word family or phonogram _____ back and find the letters of the phonogram _____ (point to them). **Place them next to the letter(s) _____ to make the word _____** (insert a sentence here using the target word). **Great, I see** (insert child's name) **has this one correct. Please spell _____ for us. Does everyone hear the /____/ sound? Let's say _____ together. Come spell _____ using the pocket chart.**

Now you have used all of the target phonograms to create words with the sound /b/ in this lesson. Instruct students to take out their "Working with Words" notebooks and write down the words they created during the lesson. Next, have students write each word in an original sentence.

T: **Class, everyone did a great job with this activity today. Let's take out our "Working with Words" notebooks and write down the words you created today.** Think of a word that was not spelled today but can be spelled using one of the phonograms you used today. Ask students to spell the word. **As you write each word, remember to say each word to yourself and listen for the _____ sound. After you write down the words, use each one in a sentence.**

Appendix B Word Card Letters

Duplicate these letters so that they are copied front to back with a lowercase letter on one side and an uppercase letter on the other. Laminate and cut out the letters for students.

a	a	a	a
e	e	e	e
i	i	i	i
o	o	o	o
u	u	u	u
y	y	y	y

c	c	b	b
f	f	d	d
h	h	g	g
k	k	j	j
m	m	l	l
p	p	n	n
r	r	q	q

t	t	s	s
w	w	v	v
z	z	x	x

Duplicate these letters so that they are copied front to back with a lowercase letter on one side and an uppercase letter on the other. Laminate and cut out the letters for students.

A	A	A	A
E	E	E	E
I	I	I	I
O	O	O	O
U	U	U	U
Y	Y	Y	Y

B	B	C	C
D	D	F	F
G	G	H	H
J	J	K	K
L	L	M	M
N	N	P	P
Q	Q	R	R

S	S	T	T
V	V	W	W
X	X	Z	Z

Duplicate these common phonograms for use in the "Working with
Words" activities.

ay	ill	ip
at	am	ag
ack	ank	ick
ell	ot	ing
ap	unk	ail
y	out	ug
op	in	an

est	ed	ab
eed	ain	ink
ore	ew	ow
ob	ock	ake
im	ight	ine
uck	um	

Appendix C The Sounds Represented by the Letters

A summary of the major sounds and generalizations follow. The summary is presented letter-by-letter in alphabetical order so you can review the sounds represented by the letters. Refer to the Table of Contents to locate lesson plans for specific sounds and generalizations.

A

The letter *a* represents six different sounds. It usually represents /ă/ when it is in a closed syllable, as in *pack*. The long sound of *a* is usually represented by *a* in syllables or words that end in a silent *e*, such as *cake* or the second syllable of *parade*. A also represents /ā/ in *ay* or *ai* combinations (as in *day* and *rain*), or when *a* is in an open syllable (as in *paper* or *baby*). When the vowel *a* precedes *r*, the sound can either be /är/, as in *car* and *arm*, or /âr/ as in *care* and *fare*. In some dialects, *a* represents broad *a* when it precedes *l*, *u*, or *w*, as in *tall*, *haul*, and *saw*. The letter *a* can represent the schwa sound, as in *banana*, *ago*, and *again*. The letter *a* is usually silent in *ea* combinations, as in *eat*, *bread*, *earth*, and *ear*, and in the *oa* combination, as in *boat*. Common phonograms with *a* include *ay*, *at*, *am*, *ag*, *ack*, *ank*, *ap*, *ail*, *an*, *ab*, and *ake*.

B

The letter *b* represents /b/ in both the initial and final positions of words, as in *bad* and *cub*. The letter *b* can be combined with either *l* or *r* to form a consonant blend, as in *black* and *brick*. When two *b*s are together in a word, as in *rubber*, the first *b* is heard and the second is silent. *B* is silent in the *mb* combinations at the end of words, as in *comb* and *lamb*.

C

The letter *c* does not represent one particular sound. *C* usually represents /k/ when it precedes *a*, *o*, or *u*, as in *cake*, *cot*, or *cut*. The letter *c* represents /s/ when it precedes *e*, *i*, or *y*, as in *cent*, *city*, or *cycle*, and can be combined with *l* or *r* to form consonant blends, as in *club* or *cross*. *C* is silent in the *ck* combination, as in *lock* and *kick*. When double *c*s appear in a word, usually the first is silent and the second is /k/, as in *account*; however, if the double *c*s are followed by *e* or *i*, the first *c* represents /k/ and the second is /s/, as in *accident*. The letter *c* is also combined with *h* to form a consonant digraph. The consonant digraph *ch* usually represents /ch/, as in *church* and *choice*; however, it can be /k/, as in *chord*, or /sh/ as in *chef*.

D

The letter *d* can represent /d/ in both the initial and final positions of words, as in *dad*. When two *d*s appear together, the first is heard and the second is silent, as in *ladder*. *D* can also be combined with *r* to *w* to form consonant blends, as in *draw* and *dwell*; it is blended with *n* in the *nd* combination in the final position of words, as in *find*.

E

The letter *e* represents five sounds: /ĕ/, as in *egg*, when it is in a closed syllable; /ē/ when it appears in the *ee*, *ea*, *ei*, *ie*, or *ey* combination, as in *bee*, *eat*, *receive*, *yield*, and *key*, or when the syllable or word ends with a silent *e*, as in *eve*. When *e* precedes *r* it represents either /ēr/, as in *her*, or /ê/, as in *here*. The letter *e* can be combined with *w* to represent /ū/, as in *few*. Finally, the letter *e* can represent the schwa sound, as in *telephone*. The letter *e* is usually silent in *ue* combinations, as in *blue*, and in words or syllables with two vowels, one of which is a final, silent *e*, as in *like*, *bake*, *cute*, and *pole*. Common phonograms with *e* include *ell*, *eed*, *est*, *ew*, and *ed*.

F

The letter *f* represents /f/ in both the initial and final positions of words, as in *family* and *if*. The *f* can be blended with *l* or *r*, as in *flag* and *from*, or with *t* in the final position of a word or syllable, as in *left*. When two *f*s appear together, the first is usually heard and the second is silent, as in *offer*.

G

G can be heard in both the initial and final positions of words, as in *gas* and *beg*. The letter *g* usually represents /g/ when it precedes *a*, *o*, or *u*. Sometimes it represents /j/ when it is followed by *e*, *i*, or *y*, as in *gem*, *giant*,

and *gym*. If two *g*s appear together in a word, the first one is usually heard and the second is silent, as in *bigger*. The letter *g* is silent in *gn* combinations, as in *gnaw* and *sign*, and can be combined with either *l* or *r* to form consonant blends, as in *glad* and *grab*.

H

The letter *h* represents /h/ in the initial position of words, as in *he* and *hat*. It is silent in the *gh* and *rh* combinations at the beginning of words, as in *ghost* and *rhyme*. The letter *h* appears in five of the six consonant digraphs: *ch*, *sh*, voiced *th*, voiceless *th*, and *wh*.

I

The letter *i* usually represents /ĭ/ in closed syllables, as in *hid* or *drip*. The letter *i* represents /ī/ when it is in an open syllable or the word ends with a silent *e*, as in *bike* or *pine*. The letter *i* can also represent the long *i* sound when it is followed by *nd*, *ght*, or *ld*, as in *mind*, *bright*, and *mild*. The sound of the letter *i* is modified by the letter *r*; when followed by *r* it usually sounds like /ēr/, as in *fir*, or /ê/, as in *irrigate*. The letter *i* can also represent the schwa sound, as in *clarity*. The letter *i* is usually silent in the *ai*, *ie*, *ei*, and *ui* combinations, as in *rain*, *piece*, *receive*, and *fruit*. The letter *i* can serve as the consonant /y/, as in *onion* and *junior*. Common phonograms with *i* include *ill*, *ip*, *ick*, *ing*, *in*, *ink*, *ine*, *ight*, and *im*.

J

The letter *j* represents /j/ in the initial position of words, as in *jar* and *joke*. The letter *j* is never found in the final position of words; however, the combination *dge* represents /j/ in the final position of words, as in *lodge* and *fudge*.

K

The letter *k* represents /k/ in the initial and final positions of words, as in *kick*. The letter *k* can also be combined with *s* to form a consonant blend, as in *skate*, and with *n* to form the *nk* blend in the final position, as in *ink*. The letter *k* is silent in the *kn* combination, as in *knot* and *know*.

L

The letter *l* represents /l/ in both the initial and final positions, as in *laugh* and *pile*. When two *l*s appear together, the first is usually heard and the second is silent, as in *jelly*. The letter *l* is found in many consonant blends, as in *black*, *clown*, *flag*, *glad*, *plan*, *slid*, *splash*, *belt*, *cold*, and *help*. It can also be found in combinations with the letter *a* representing the broad *a* sound, as in *ball* and *talk*.

M

The letter *m* represents /m/ in both the initial and final positions, as in *mad* and *ham*. When two *m*s appear together, the first is usually heard and the second is silent, as in *summer*. Consonant blends are formed with *sm*, as in *small*, and when *m* and *p* are together, as in *camp*.

N

The letter *n* represents /n/ in both the initial and final positions, as in *name* and *can*. When two *n*s appear together, the first is usually heard and the second is silent, as in *winner*. The letter *n* is found in some consonant blends, as in *snail*, *ant*, and *and*. It is also found in the /ng/ consonant digraph, as in *ring*.

O

The letter *o* can represent as many as eight different vowel sounds, depending on the position and combination with other letters. The letter *o* usually represents /ŏ/ when it is in a closed syllable, as in *hop* or *dog*. The letter *o* represents /ō/ in open syllables, as in *go*, and in the *oa* combination, as in *boat*. The letter *o* also represents /ō/ when *o* is followed by *ld*, as in *gold*, or if the syllable or word has a final silent *e*, as in *joke*. Sometimes the letter *o* is combined with *u* or *w* to represent the diphthong /ou/, as in *cow*; at other times *ow* represents /ō/, as in *low*. The letter *o* is also combined with *i* to represent the /oi/ diphthong, as in *oil*. When the letter *o* precedes *r*, it usually represents /ôr/, as in *organ*; however, it can represent /ēr/ in the final syllable of multi-syllabic words, as in *color* and *doctor*. When two *o*s appear together in a word, they represent either /ōō/, as in *tool*, or /ŏŏ/, as in *book*. Of course the letter *o* can represent the schwa sound, as in *octopus*. Finally, the letter *o* can represent /ŭ/, as in *won*, *some*, and *rough*. Common phonograms with *o* include *ot*, *out*, *op*, *ow*, *ore*, *ob*, and *ock*.

P

The letter *p* represents /p/ in the initial and final positions of syllables and words, as in *pep*. The letter *p* can also be combined with *l* or *r* to form consonant blends, as in *play* or *print*. The *lp* and *mp* blends are found in the final position of some syllables and words, as in *help* and *chimp*. The letter *p* also appears in the three-letter consonant blends *spl* (as in *splash*) and *spr* (as in *spring*). When it is combined with *h*, the *ph* generally represents /f/, as in *phone*. When two *ps* occur together, the first is usually heard and the second is silent, as in *happy*. The letter *p* is usually silent when it precedes *n*, *s*, or *t* at the beginning of words, as in *pneumonia*, *psalm*, and *ptomaine*.

Q

Q does not have a sound of its own, but usually is followed by *u* to represent the /kw/ blend, as in *quiet* or *quilt*. *Q* also represents /k/, as in *antique*. The *qu* combination is found in a three-letter blend with the letter *s*, as in *squash*.

R

The letter *r* represents a consonant sound, as in *run*. When the letter *r* is preceded by a vowel, the vowel sound is modified by the *r*—as in *cär*, *câre*, *hẽr*, *hêre*, and *ôrgan*. The letter *r* is found in many consonant blends, as in *brace*, *cream*, *dream*, *free*, *great*, *print*, *tree*, *string*, and *throw*.

S

The letter *s* can represent /s/ in both the initial and final positions of syllables and words, as in *saw* and *us*; however, it also represents /z/ in the final position of many words, as in *has*. The letter *s* is a part of numerous consonant blends, as in *scold*, *school*, *skate*, *scrub*, *shrill*, *slow*, *small*, *snail*, *speak*, *sphere*, *splash*, *spring*, *squash*, *stop*, *string*, *sway*, *last*, *wasp*, and *lisp*. When double *ss* appear in a word, the first is usually heard and the second is silent, as in *blossom*. The letter *s* can also be combined with the letter *h* to form the consonant digraph *sh*, as in *share*. The letter *s* can also represent /sh/, as in *sugar* and *sure*.

T

The letter *t* represents /t/ in both the initial and final positions of syllables and words, as in *tot*. The letter *t* is also found in many consonant blends, as in *tractor*, *twice*, *left*, *belt*, *went*, *last*, *start*, and *string*. When two *ts* appear together, the first is usually heard and the second is silent, as in *better*. The letter *t* is silent in *often* and other words that end in *ten*, such as *fasten*. The letter *t* is also silent in the *stle* combination, as in *castle*, and the *tch* combination, as in *catch*. The letter *t* is combined with *h* to form two digraphs: voiced *th*, as in *that*, and voiceless *th*, as in *thin*. The voiceless *th* can be combined with *r* to form a consonant blend, as in *threw*, *three*, and *throat*.

U

The letter *u* can represent the short *u* sound, as in *tub*, and the long *u* sound, as in *use*. The *u* usually represents /ŭ/ in closed syllables, as in *bun*, while *u* is /ū/ in open syllables, as in *hula, judo,* and *ruin.* The letter *u* usually represents /ū/ when it is in a word or syllable that has a final *e,* such as *tube* or *truce.* When *u* precedes *r,* the vowel sound is /ēr/, as in *burn.* The letter *u* can be combined with *o* to form the *ou* diphthong, as in *ouch.* The letter *u* is silent when it follows *g* and precedes another vowel at the beginning of words, as in *guess.* Of course, the letter *u* can represent the schwa sound, as in *focus.* Finally the letter *u* always follows *q* to represent /kw/ (as in *quiet*) or /k/ (as in *croquet*). Common phonograms with *u* include *unk, ug, uck,* and *um.*

V

The letter *v* can represent /v/ in both the initial and final positions of words and syllables, as in *voice* and *have.* The letter *v* is one of the most consistent letters in American English in its representation of a particular sound.

W

The consonant sound of *w* is heard at the beginning of words, as in *went.* The letter *w* also is combined with vowels to represent vowel sounds, as in *law, cow,* and *few.* The letter *w* is also found in consonant blends, as in *dwell, swim,* and *twin.* The letter *w* is silent in *wr* combinations, as in *wrap* and *wrote.* The letter *w* is found in the consonant digraph *wh* to represent /hw/, as in *whale.* When *wh* is followed by *o,* as in *who,* the *w* is silent.

X

The letter *x* does not have its own sound; however, it represents /eks/ as in *box,* /eks/ as in *excuse,* /z/ as in *xylophone,* and /gz/ as in *examination.*

Y

The letter *y* represents the consonant sound /y/ at the beginning of a few words, as in *yo-yo;* however, it usually represents a vowel sound. The letter *y* can represent /ĭ/ in closed syllables, as in *gym,* and it represents the /ī/ sound at the end of syllables and words in which *y* is the only vowel, as in *xylophone* and *by.* The letter *y* can also represent the long *e* sound or the short *i* sound at the end of multisyllabic words, as in *happy.* *Y* is combined with *o* to represent the /oi/ diphthong, as heard in *boy.* The letter *y* is silent in *ay* and *ey* combinations, as in *day* and *key.*

Z

The letter *z* represents /z/ and can be found in both initial and final positions of words, as in *zoo* and *jazz.* The letter *z* also represents /zh/, as in *seizure.*

Glossary

Accent: Emphasis given to a syllable in pronouncing a word. A syllable that has a primary accent is pronounced more emphatically than a syllable with a secondary accent. In the word *vacation*, the syllable /kā/ has a primary accent and the first syllable, /vā/, has a secondary accent.

Blending: The gliding or shaping of one sound into another.

Closed Syllable: A syllable ending in a consonant. Generally the vowel sound in closed syllables is short, as in *bat*.

Consonant: A speech sound produced by the obstruction or blocking of the free passage of air in the oral cavity. Twenty-four consonant sounds are described in this book.

Consonant Blend: Diffusion of two or more sounds into one sound without the identity of either sound being lost, as in the blend of *t* and *r* in *tree*. A consonant blend is not considered a new speech sound, as is a consonant digraph; rather, it is simply the blending of two existing sounds.

Consonant Cluster: A group of two or more consonant letters that represent one speech sound, as in *dge* represents /j/ in *badge*. A consonant cluster may represent a new speech sound (digraph), be a blend of two or more consonants, or represent a sound that is usually represented in another way (as when *ph*—instead of *f*—represents /f/).

Consonant Digraph: A single speech sound represented by two consonant letters, resulting in a new sound rather than a blending of the sounds of the two consonants. The consonant digraphs in this books are *ch*, *sh*, *ng*, voiced *th*, voiceless *th*, and *wh*.

Consonant Trigraph: A combination of three consonants representing one sound—for example, *str* in string.

Context Clues: Clues to the pronunciation or meaning of a word that are derived by analyzing the words preceding or following the unknown word.

Diphthong: A sound produced by gliding from one vowel sound to another, resulting in a single speech sound; an example is the /oi/ sound in *oil*.

Double Consonants: Two like consonants appearing together in a word or syllable. In most double consonants the first consonant is heard and the second is silent, as in *hammer*.

Final Consonant Blend: A combination of consonant letters occurring at the end of a word or syllable that are blended in pronunciation, and thus represent one speech sound. Examples include *nd* and *lt*, as in *find* and *belt*.

Open Syllable: A syllable ending with a vowel. Generally the vowel has a long sound in an open syllable, as in *go*.

Phoneme or Sound: A single speech sound. For example, /b/ is a phoneme.

Phoneme–Grapheme Relationship: The relationship of consonant and vowel sounds to the written symbols that represent them. The phoneme for *b* is /b/; the grapheme is *b*. The term *sound–symbol relationship* is a synonym for *phoneme–grapheme relationship*.

Phonetic Analysis: The analysis of sound units in an unknown word as a means of pronouncing the word, and deriving its meaning by relating this pronunciation to one's listening vocabulary. The term *phonics* is often used as a synonym for phonetic analysis.

Phonetics: The science of speech sounds, including the study of sound formation through positioning of the lips, tongue, and jaw, and through other speech mechanisms.

Phonics: The use of speech sounds and sound–symbol relationships to help the student achieve independence in the recognition of words.

Phonogram: A combination of a vowel and consonant(s) that appear together frequently as in *ay, ill, at, am,* and *ip*. Synonyms for phonograms are sound patterns or word families.

Reinforcement Activity: An activity designed to give the learner an opportunity to practice or apply a skill to make it strong in his or her mind. The ultimate objects of reinforcement activities is application at the automatic-response level.

R-Modified Sounds: The vowel sounds that result when the letter *r* follows a vowel, as in *car, care, her, here, fir, irrigate, burn,* and *organ*.

Schwa Sound: A faint, indistinct vowel sound that is only slightly heard in the unstressed syllable of a multisyllabic word. All the vowel letters can represent the schwa sound. The schwa sound is also called the *neutralized sound* and is heard in *around, telephone, multiply, revolution,* and *saturate*.

Sight Words: Words recognized as a whole rather than through the analysis of their parts. Sight words are usually words that a child can recognize within three seconds without analysis.

Silent *e* Principle: The principle or generalization that when a word or syllable ends in a final *e*, the final *e* is usually silent, and the preceding vowel is usually long, as in *like* and *arrange*.

Silent Letter: A letter or group of letters that are not pronounced in a word. In the *kn* combination, *k* is silent, as in *knight* and *knife*. The silent letters in *light* are *g* and *h*.

Sound Pattern: A combination of a vowel and consonants that appear together frequently. Sample sound patterns are *ay, ill, at, am,* and *ip*.

Sound–Symbol Relationship: The relationship of a sound to its written symbol. For example, /d/ is represented by *d*. A synonym for this term is *phoneme–grapheme relationship*.

Structural Analysis: Analyzing words to determine prefixes, suffixes, inflectional endings, or other parts, in order to recognize the whole word. In recognizing the word *redo*, you can analyze the structure by identifying the prefix *re* and the root word *do*.

Syllabification or Syllabication: The act of dividing words into groups of letters known as syllables.

Syllable: One or more speech sound that represents a complete articulation and forms either a whole word or part of a word.

Voiced: Describes speech sounds accompanied by tones resulting from the vibration of the vocal folds.

Voiceless or Unvoiced: Describes speech sounds spoken without tones resulting from the vibration of vocal folds.

Vowel: A sound produced through the vibrations of the vocal chords by the air passing relatively unobstructed through the oral part of the breath channel.

Vowel Digraph: A combination of two vowel letters representing one speech sound, such as the *ea* in *heat*.

Word-Pronunciation Strategy: The procedures the reader uses to determine the correct pronunciation of a word. The word-pronunciation strategy might include looking for affixes, dividing the word into syllables, looking for sound patterns, determining the sounds the various letters represent, using context clues, or locating the word in a dictionary.

Word Recognition: The process of perceiving words while reading and associating meaning with them.